OCTOBER BIRDS

Social Fictions Series

Series Editor
Patricia Leavy
USA

The *Social Fictions* series emerges out of the arts-based research movement. The series includes full-length fiction books that are informed by social research but written in a literary/artistic form (novels, plays, and short story collections). Believing there is much to learn through fiction, the series only includes works written entirely in the literary medium adapted. Each book includes an academic introduction that explains the research and teaching that informs the book as well as how the book can be used in college courses. The books are underscored with social science or other scholarly perspectives and intended to be relevant to the lives of college students—to tap into important issues in the unique ways that artistic or literary forms can.

Please email queries to pleavy7@aol.com

October Birds

A Novel about Pandemic Influenza, Infection
Control and First Responders

By

Jessica Smartt Gullion
Department of Sociology and Social Work, Texas Woman's University, USA

SENSE PUBLISHERS
ROTTERDAM / BOSTON / TAIPEI

A C.I.P. record for this book is available from the Library of Congress.

ISBN 978-94-6209-588-5 (paperback)
ISBN 978-94-6209-589-2 (hardback)
ISBN 978-94-6209-590-8 (e-book)

Published by: Sense Publishers,
P.O. Box 21858, 3001 AW Rotterdam, The Netherlands
https://www.sensepublishers.com/

Printed on acid-free paper

TABLE OF CONTENTS

ACKNOWLEDGMENTS

A project of this scope does not happen in isolation. First and foremost, I would like to thank Sense Publishers Social Fiction Series Editor Patricia Leavy for her support of this book. Its publication came about by a strange synchronicity that will be a story I'll tell forever. Thank you also to Peter de Liefde and everyone at Sense Publishers.

The initial draft of this story was written during National Novel Writing Month (www.nanowrimo.org). I have to give a big thanks to all of the folks involved in that project. Because of your work I'll never be a 'one day' novelist again.

Thanks to my first readers, Dona Perkins and Elrena Evans.

Finally, thanks to Greg, Renn, and Rory. You are my love and my light.

PREFACE

October Birds was born in the overlapping space between science and art.

In 2003, in the wake of 9/11 and the anthrax letters, I was hired to be the Chief Epidemiologist of one of the largest county public health departments in Texas. The funds for my position originated through federal concern over bioterrorism, and I was tasked with planning and preparing for bioterror response. Luckily, it didn't happen.

Overtime, bioterrorism seemed less an immediate threat, and public health became increasingly concerned with emerging and reemerging infectious diseases. The SARS outbreak was a frightening realization of what could happen. Ease of world travel, coupled with a susceptible population, are kindling for a new infectious disease. People were put into isolation and quarantine, and public health legal powers were used to a level many of us have never seen.

SARS died out, but while the experience was fresh, public health professions wondered what would have happened had the SARS fire blazed more widely.

Another likely scenario to consider, similar in nature to SARS, was pandemic influenza. A pandemic is a world-wide disease outbreak. Our statistical models, based in part on SARS and on the 1918 Spanish Flu pandemic, were frightening. I spent a good portion of my work days strategizing and writing response plans for coping with such a catastrophe.

And then it happened.

In the spring of 2009, I began to receive reports of unusual flu activity. A new strain of flu, an Influenza A (H1N1) – dubbed 'swine flu' by the press – emerged in Texas and California. Was this the pandemic we'd prepared for? We had no idea how deadly this flu would be. Fortunately, it turned out to be relatively mild, but we had no way to predict that. For a while, public health responded as if our fears had materialized. We took many of the actions portrayed in *October Birds*. While our goal was to prevent as much illness and death as possible, we were accused of over-response and our actions criticized.

While a work of fiction, *October Birds* is grounded in real-life public health practice, sociological research, and emergency management. The novel a/r/tographical research, a sociological inquiry within the science/art intersection. This novel is an accumulation of my knowledge and experiences with infectious disease outbreaks. I draw on scientific literature from medical, infection control, public health, and sociology journals. I also draw on personal experience. Many of the scenarios in the novel, while fictionalized, are based on actual events. But *October Birds* is more than a story – it is also a sociological theory of community-level response to health threats. Using fiction as a mode of representation, I hope to reach a larger audience than I could by focusing on a traditional academic one, a goal important to me as an applied sociologist.

I believe that in writing social fiction, we also engage in the writing of social theory. This work is a representation of my theorizing on community-level health threats, from the perspective of public health, hospitals, and emergency services.

A community-level health threat is one in which every member of the community is theoretically susceptible. While pathology may vary person-to-person, all residents are threatened. I have fourteen years' experience as an applied sociologist, helping communities cope with such threats. I have worked on outbreaks of vaccine-preventable disease (such as whooping cough and rubella), food borne outbreaks (including contaminated vegetables and peanut butter), contaminated medical devices, flesh-eating bacteria, and other diseases. I have also run and managed shelters for people fleeing natural disasters (including Hurricane Katrina), and have assisted in disaster recovery. Four years ago, I joined the sociology faculty at Texas Woman's University. While I am actively engaged in a research agenda on community-level health threats, I have shifted my focus from infectious disease to environmental health threats, such as from toxins in the air and water, and I research and teach on these issues.

October Birds takes place in the fictional city of Dalton, Texas. Using a hypothetical population of 115,000, I conducted statistical modeling to project morbidity and mortality rates similar to the 1918 Spanish Flu pandemic. Each chapter is equivalent to about one week of the outbreak. Dalton has one hospital – Memorial – and I used my knowledge of mid-sized regional hospitals to construct it. The number of beds, ventilators, and negative air-flow rooms is about what is typical for this size hospital. Patient overflow, shelters, and points of dispensing medication are all likely to be found in most disaster plans.

Dalton has a city health department with infectious disease and disaster professions. Most cities are not so well-staffed in reality, but it was necessary for the story. It is more likely that this size department would serve an entire county or perhaps even region of a state.

While I find the technical details interesting, it is the social interactions which make community-level health threats interesting. The medical sociology literature is ripe with research on power and dominance in the medical profession, patterns which play out in the novel. Clashes between licensed healthcare professionals and traditional healers are well-documented in the literature as well. No matter how prepared a community is for disaster, things go wrong. Professionals and volunteers responding to the event become overwhelmed and they burn out. Their mental health is often overlooked in the midst of the response. These themes and others are explored in the novel.

Fiction was used in the very first sociology course I took, and I use fiction in courses I teach today. Through fiction, we can imagine alternatives to our current social structure. We can explore what happens when the structures that seem concrete crumble around us. We can answer the question: 'What if?' using sociological research and practice.

This novel can be read as a supplementary text in a number of disciplines, including sociology (such as in courses on collective behavior or medical sociology); nursing, public health, and health studies; emergency management; and psychology (in courses on critical incident stress management and crisis counseling). It can also be used interdisciplinarily in courses on qualitative research methods. I hope it will also be read simply for pleasure, and instill the question: 'What if?' What if a devastating pandemic does emerge? How will we respond as a society? The question is real. Recent reports on Pro-MED (the Program for Monitoring Emerging Diseases, www.promedmail.org) on avian influenza in Asia hint at the possibility of a new pandemic. How will we respond?

Jessica Smartt Gullion

INTRODUCTION

"What's next on the board?"

Dr Stratford leaned against the large U-shaped desk and looked for his nurse. The heart patient (chief complaint: chest pain, history of stent) had been referred to the on-call cardiologist and the attempted suicide (chief complaint: drug overdose) sat moaning to the hospital psychologist about how her boyfriend had dumped her via text message. Her throat still sounded hoarse from the stomach pumping. He tried not to be rough with them, the suicides, but it really pissed him off, having to spend time saving someone who wanted to die while other patients waited for his attention, scared, hurting, or just plain ready to get out of the emergency room and on with their lives.

"You've got a five year old with a fever in exam room one. Adult male complaining of vomiting and jaundiced in room two. Wait till you see his eyes, they're freakishly yellow. His wife's all upset, she's being belligerent. I can't get a good history from her. Her English is terrible," the nurse said. He opted for the kid.

The child lay still on the exam table, folded into a curl on his side, his eyes closed. His mother swiveled on the rolling stool, turning her hips from side to side, holding on to his hand. Dr Stratford liked working with kids. He had almost become a pediatrician, but he loved the adrenaline and drama of the emergency room even more.

"You look like you don't feel well," Dr Stratford said. The boy opened his eyes and stared at him. They were an old man's eyes, dark and tired. His cheeks and ears had a bright scarlet hue.

"He's been running a fever all day. A hundred and three at the highest," the mother said. She placed her palm on the boy's forehead for emphasis.

"Any other symptoms? Coughing? Sore throat?"

"No, nothing." She shot Dr Stratford a concerned look, and then her eyes darted away, not wanting to prolong eye contact with the doctor. A lot of people did that.

"Hey buddy. Can you sit up?" Dr Stratford put his stethoscope in his ears and warmed up the base with his hands while the boy reluctantly, and rather dramatically, sat up in a slouch.

"Just breath in normally," Dr Stratford said. The boy's lungs sounded clear. Healthy. No problems with the heart, that sounded fine. He looked into the boy's eyes. "Watch my finger without moving your head." The boy's eyes followed, up, down, to either side.

"Can you touch your chin to your chest? Like this?" Dr Stratford demonstrated. The boy bent his neck. "Does that hurt at all? No?

"What about your tummy? Does your tummy hurt?" The boy shook his head no. "Can you lay down? Let me check it?"

The boy lay back and curled himself into a ball. Dr Stratford gently rolled him onto his back and straightened out his legs.

"I just don't know what's wrong with him. He's been acting really tired all day. He says nothing hurts, but then there's this fever. I don't know what to do."

"It sounds like you are doing all of the right things. Does this hurt?" He palpitated the boy's abdomen. Everything felt fine. No obstructions. No abscesses. "Does it hurt when you go potty? When you pee?" The boy shook his head.

"I'm going to move your legs around, ok? Do they hurt? Does it hurt when you walk?" He bent the boy's legs at the knee and then pushed them into his abdomen. The boy had no signs of meningitis. His cell phone rang. "Excuse me for just a minute," he said to the mother.

"Your patient over in room two is not looking so hot," the nurse told him. "His wife is demanding you get in there."

"Ok," he replied. He hung up on her. The man could wait.

"Did they give him any fever medicine in triage?" he asked the mother.

"No," she said. That irritated him. A child with fever; they were supposed to give Tylenol, start to make him comfortable instead of making him suffer while waiting to be seen.

"Alright. We'll get him some Tylenol and some Motrin. I want you to give him both, alternating every three hours. Tylenol.

Wait three hours. Motrin. Wait three hours. Then Tylenol again. Ok? If he doesn't get better in a couple of days, see his pediatrician." He watched the boy curl himself up again. "This looks like a viral infection, nothing serious, but keep an eye on him. If he gets worse, bring him back. If he develops any more symptoms, call your pediatrician or just bring him back. We are here to help. The nurse will bring you a print out of instructions, things to watch for. Do you have any questions?"

"No, I don't think so. I was really worried about meningitis. You don't think it's meningitis?"

"No. He doesn't have signs of it."

"Thank you for looking at him."

"I'll have the nurse bring you some medicine and then you can take him home, ok?"

Outside the exam room, Dr Stratford pumped the alcohol-based hand sanitizer from the wall-mounted container and cleaned his hands. A burning sensation reminded him of the small cut he'd gotten earlier, scraped it while scrambling on the heart patient. An intense burning sensation. He found his nurse working a crossword puzzle. "If it's not too much trouble, get the kid in exam one four mills each of Tylenol and Motrin."

"Four mills each? That seems high," she said.

He glared at her.

"Besides," she continued, "we only have infant Tylenol, not children's. You'll have to order it from pharmacy." She filled a word in to her puzzle.

He took a deep breath and told himself to relax. "Are you telling me that we are an emergency room and we can't give a kid with a fever some Tylenol?"

"That's right," she said, looking up from her puzzle. "You'll have to order it from pharmacy."

"I have worked in this emergency room for fifteen years," he said, his voice rising. "And in that time I have seen thousands of kids with fevers and I have given them all Tylenol. And now you are telling me that that is not how things work in my ER?" He realized he had caught the attention of most of the people in the room. "Get the kid the Tylenol. Now."

The nurse sat debating for a moment whether or not to fight with him, rolled her eyes, and stormed off in search of the medicine.

"What a bitch."

Dr Stratford looked up to see his friend, Benjamin Cromwell. "She's new," Stratford said.

"Where'd they get her?" Dr Cromwell asked him.

"Who knows? Damn nursing shortage. They'll scrape the bottom of the barrel for whatever they can get," Dr Stratford said. Frankly, the whole thing sickened him. He missed the days when nurses did what they were told. Nowadays they questioned him, double-guessed him, constantly.

Finished with the boy, he started to check on his patient in exam two.

The ambulance bay doors burst open. Two EMTs rushed in, pushing a man on a gurney. "He's crashing!" one of them yelled. "Respiratory distress. We intubated him in the box."

Dr Stratford ran after them, his adrenaline rising.

CHAPTER 1

Dalton, Texas
Total infected = 1
Total dead = 0

"I have Japanese Encephalitis," a woman on the phone told her.

"Really? Have you been to a doctor?" Eliza scratched the letters JE on her purple notepad and began to take the report.

"No, I just think, I mean, I am pretty sure that's what I have."

"Ok. Why do you think that? Have you traveled outside of the country recently?"

"No, I think I must be the first person to get it in the United States. I looked up my symptoms on the internet and that sounds exactly like what I have."

Eliza rubbed her temples and tried not to sigh audibly into the phone. She hated people who self-diagnosed. Especially off of the internet. No one ever diagnosed themselves with something benign. No, they were all dying of something exotic that would awe their friends. "You really need to go to the doctor for a diagnosis," she said.

"Can you just do a blood test for me?"

"What are your symptoms?" Eliza asked.

"Well, I've had this really bad headache off and on for a few weeks now and my muscles all hurt. Oh, and I've been nauseated."

"Have you had a fever?"

"No."

"There are a lot of things that can cause those symptoms. It is important that you see a doctor because the doctor can find out what is going on and can help you." She drew spirals down the side of her paper. She smelled coffee; Geoff must be in. She could always trust Geoff to brew a pot.

"Oh. Ok. So you can't just test my blood?"

"If your doctor decides that you might have Japanese Encephalitis, we will be happy to work with them to get your blood tested for it. But I need to talk with the doctor about that first." She wanted to add, and leave me alone, you kook, but didn't.

1

"Oh, Ok. Well, thanks."

The voice really didn't sound thankful. Eliza hung up the phone and went to get some coffee. On the way down the hall she noticed that her cup had mold at the bottom.

For the last few years, Dr Elizabeth Gordon had worked as Chief Epidemiologist of the City of Dalton Public Health Department. She headed up the Disease Investigation Unit. She had two investigators, Geoffrey Robins, who she thought was wonderful, and Julia Campos, who she wished would quit. She was indifferent about Lucy, her administrative assistant. The Disease Investigation Unit conducted reports on communicable disease (fortunately not sexually transmitted ones – Eliza hated dealing with STDs – that was handled by another division). Most of their time was spent talking with people about their food poisoning or tracking down children with pertussis. The investigators interviewed the patients, asked them questions about their illness, where they thought they got sick, who else they might have exposed, and whatnot. Eliza did not like to talk to members of the general public, and avoided talking to patients whenever possible. She talked to the healthcare providers, the doctors, the nurses, the people working in the labs; that was more her element. They spoke the same language and she didn't have to explain everything to them. And they didn't assume they were all dying of some tropical disease.

Geoff was already at the sink, rinsing out his own cup. "Morning, Dr E."

"Morning," she replied. "Why is it that every crazy person in this city has my phone number?"

He laughed. "It's too early for crazy."

"Amen to that."

"So what's on the agenda for today, boss?" he asked.

"I still have to pull the lab reports off the server," she said. "Did you call Evers Elementary back about their kindergartener with pertussis?"

"Yeah, I finished that one up yesterday. The kid has been treated and everyone in the family all received antibiotics. The school nurse was supposed to have sent a letter home to parents yesterday. I'll call her this morning to make sure it actually went out."

Eliza stirred a spoonful of fat-free hazelnut flavored creamer into her coffee and wished she was at home, asleep. Sophie woke her up crying at 3am after she wet the bed. Poor Sophie had pee all over herself, even in her hair, and Eliza had to give her a bath. Sophie cried. Afterward, Eliza let her crawl up into bed with her. Her husband Steven slept through the whole ordeal.

Back at her desk, 134 emails waited for Eliza to read them. Most were junk, she just deleted them, but it was time consuming nonetheless. One caught her attention: a Pro-MED posting, someone wanting information on an outbreak in Indonesia. Pro-MED is an international email list public health folks used for reporting and discussing disease outbreaks. She told her boss that she monitored it to keep tabs on outbreaks in other parts of the world that could impact the citizens of Dalton, but really, she just thought it was interesting. Unusual diseases in Dalton almost always originated in another country, brought back as an unfortunate vacation souvenir. Eliza liked travel medicine; it gave her a chance to see real cases of unusual diseases. Most of their travel-related disease cases came from the university. The anthropology department was particularly prone to tropical disease. Those kids liked to backpack through the most primitive conditions they could find, but they hated taking their malaria pills. The pills gave them gastrointestinal problems, and who wanted to be sick on vacation? Many of them came home with a raging case of malaria as a result. This report, however, was not on malaria. It was a request for information on a rumor: a large number of people in Jakarta were reportedly sick with pneumonia, and they were dropping like flies.

That was how SARS started. Rumors back and forth on Pro-MED. A bunch of patients in China with pneumonia. High mortality. Cause unknown. The Chinese government denying anything was going on. She forwarded the email to Jack over in the Public Health Preparedness Division, with a brief note, "Job Security?"

3

The small clapboard house sat in a field just outside of town. At first glance, the yard appeared a tangle of overgrown foliage. Cassandra didn't like carefully planted columns and rows; she sprinkled the seeds out and just let the plants grow as they would. Nature doesn't exist on our terms, she firmly believed that. She only pulled plants that she couldn't use – she hated the term weed and all the evil it implied – when they threatened to kill off her medicinal herbs.

An old cattle fence surrounded the property, rusted and sagging in places. The gate hung open, propped with a large clay pot filled with flowering cacti, the pot painted in blues and yellows. She wanted to be welcoming to her patients without actually advertising her clinic. Because many of her patients were not in the US legally, she didn't want to draw attention from the wrong sorts, people who wanted to send the immigrants home. Plus there were always issues with the biomedical community. They didn't approve of her and certainly didn't want her taking their business. While she had not had any trouble here in Dalton, a *curandera* in Ogden was arrested and prosecuted for practicing medicine without a license.

In the kitchen, Cassandra hung freshly cut herbs upside down from a shower curtain rod that hung along the length of the ceiling. She had opened the windows, and a cool breeze came in, filling her house with their scent. The October nights had grown cooler; this was likely to be the last harvest before winter. She tied the plants to the pole with lengths of satin ribbon. It was a pretty decoration, but functional too. Once the herbs dried, she would take them down and put them in jars, for making teas and poultices.

A battered emerald Oldsmobile turned into the drive, kicking up a dust storm. She watched the car approach, wiped her hands off on her apron, and went out on the front porch to greet the passengers. A small Hispanic woman with a river of long black hair got out of the car, walked around to the passenger side and took a child out of a car seat in the back. The child laid her head on her mother's shoulder, curling up into a comma on her chest.

Cassandra walked down the steps and over to them. Green mucus caked the child's upper lip. The girl sniffed hard, sucking some of it back into her nose. "Poor little thing. What is wrong with your baby?" Cassandra asked.

"Oh, so sick," the woman said. "So sick. Amelia say to come to you, that you could help? She say you help her to get pregnant, where her womb was too cold for baby."

"Of course, come inside and I will take a look at her. Amelia is a good friend." Cassandra relied on word-of-mouth, and had no lack of business. Word spread quickly through the immigrant communities when traditional healers were available.

Cassandra smiled and led them up to the house. The mother introduced herself, Maria, and sat her daughter down on the sofa.

The girl was about two years old, her cheeks flushed with fever. Cassandra went in the kitchen to make some tea. With the fall, the number of children coming to see her always increased. Colds with fever. Ear infections. Allergies. "She is coughing?" Cassandra called back to Maria.

"Yes, cough and running nose, so much runny nose."

"How is she sleeping?"

"She is not sleeping so good. She has too much runny nose."

Cassandra took a large piece of ginger root out of her refrigerator. She used a bit of it to make the tea and wrapped the rest in plastic wrap. She let the root steep for five minutes while she talked to the mother, and then put an ice cube in the cup so the drink would not burn the child's mouth.

"How long have you been in Dalton?" Cassandra asked. She watched as the girl considered the tea.

"A few months. My husband's brother, he has been here many year. My husband, he has been to America a few times, he has come for work. This is our first time come though."

"And what do you think of America?"

"Oh, American, this is fine." She played with the hem of her skirt. "I miss Guatemala though. You know, Guatemala, I work as accountant, I learn English. But here, here they listen you have an accent, you know? They think that you dumb, stupid for bad English. Hard finding work." She held the cup up to her daughter's lips. "I try taking her to the *Departamento de Salud,* to see doctor. That was, how you say, not a good idea. No help. No fixing her."

Cassandra nodded. She'd heard lots of complaints about the health department.

"I tell my husband, this America, it's not so good, we go back to Guatemala. But he say we should try. There is much opportunity, he say. I don't know. I think it is not what we thought. Like poor. I never knew America has poor people. But here we are. Not like I thought at all." She shrugged.

She fed the drink to her daughter slowly. The girl did not complain, but seemed to like it.

Cassandra sat next to the girl and took her head in her hands. She whispered prayers and fluttered her fingers over the girl's eyelids. Then she placed her hands over the girl's chest, again with whispered prayers. She picked up an egg that she had sat in a bowl on the coffee table. Holding the egg in her right hand, she formed the sign of the cross repeatedly over the girl's forehead and chest. "In the name of the Father, the Son, and the Holy Spirit," she said. She cracked the egg into the bowl. The vibrant yellow yolk swelled with the girl's fever.

"I will give you this root. Cut off a small piece, like this, see?" Cassandra held up the bit that she had used to make the tea. "Peel it first. Put the piece in a cup of boiling water. Once the water is cool, give it to her to drink. Give it to her at least four times every day. It should fix her right up, but if she isn't feeling any better by tomorrow afternoon, you bring her back, ok?"

Maria nodded. "Thank you, thank you so much."

She went back to the kitchen for a bottle of liquid Echinacea with a small dropper attached to the lid. "When she is done drinking the tea, give her one dropper of this." She filled the dropper and held it to the girl's mouth. When the girl opened her mouth, Cassandra squirted it inside. The girl grimaced. "It tastes awful. But it will make her stronger."

"What can I give you, to thank you?" Maria asked.

Cassandra believed that to deny people her healing abilities because they had no money was morally wrong. She let people pay what they could, what they thought her services were worth. Some could give her nothing, they had nothing themselves. It didn't bother her. She had a gift from God and God gave it to her to help people, not to make money off of them. In turn, the community supported her. They made sure she had everything she needed to survive. Some would insist on giving her money or food, or other items. She found curious gifts left on her front porch like precious orphans. Once a man gave her three chickens for curing his arthritis. It was a meager life. Meager, but fulfilling.

"No, no, nothing my friend. I only want your daughter to be well."

"Thank you, thank you," Maria said. She gathered her daughter up and carried her back out to the car. After she strapped the girl into her car seat, Maria returned with a large insulated container.

"You must take these. I make fresh this morning for you."

Cassandra opened the box to find a large batch of fluffy corn tortillas. Hand-made. Her favorite.

"I will enjoy them. God bless you."

As she watched the car drive away, she rolled up one of the tortillas and took a bite. It was still warm.

Michael hurried down the cold corridor to the intensive care unit. Dr Cromwell paged him twice. The great doctor could be a real asshole if kept waiting. Dr Cromwell was the hospital's infectious disease specialist, and as the infection control director of the facility, Michael worked with him often, especially when they had healthcare workers exposed to communicable diseases.

"Michael. I'm glad you could come," Dr Cromwell said in a flat voice. He stood in front of the nurses' station, a patient chart in his hands. "I've got an interesting one this morning."

Michael noted the patient inside the isolation room. The ventilator blew air into his lungs, inflating and deflating them in an artificial rhythm. All the tubes and wires – Michael always thought ICU patients looked inhuman. Like robots. Cyborgs.

The ICU had two negative pressure isolation rooms. They treated the critical patients with airborne communicable diseases in these rooms. The air intake inside the isolation rooms operated on its own system, separate from the rest of the hospital. The exhaust vented through special HEPA filters directly outside the building. Generally, the patients housed there had tuberculosis. Occasionally someone really sick with chickenpox. There were a few more isolation rooms in the hospital, two down on the first floor among the regular patient rooms, and two in the emergency department. One of those could hold three patients at once if need be, but they'd never had occasion for it.

A lab tech exited the room covered in full personal protective equipment. Just outside the door, she removed the paper gown and doubled gloves and threw them into a biohazard bag. Michael realized it was Donna, the lab director. He was surprised to see her here. Usually she sent one of her minions to collect specimens. She pulled off her respirator and goggles and placed them in the biohazard bag as well. Everything was disposable to minimize contamination. Still, Michael watched as she slipped up in her procedure, touching the outside of the mask with her bare hand, and contaminating herself anyway. He didn't say anything.

"What's he got?" asked Michael.

"He tested positive for influenza A."

"He's got the flu?" Good Lord, thought Michael. Why do you need me for a flu patient?

Dr Cromwell smiled a crocked smile.

"He flew in yesterday from Indonesia."

"Really?"

"Yeah. He's a physician there."

Michael scrambled to pull the meeting together. Despite his insistence about the magnitude of the situation, most of the department heads had other things to do. The Chief Nursing Officer sent a substitute, Valarie, a nurse fresh out of a master's program with little real-life experience. Dr Stratford, the emergency department director, showed though, as did the safety officer and the risk manager.

Dr Cromwell watched Michael with a mixture of pity and amusement. He found Michael pathetic, a caricature of a man, complete with a pudgy gut falling over threadbare slacks and oversized spectacles that slid down his nose. To top it off, he had an irritating habit of ending all of his sentences with a lilt in his voice, as if questioning himself on everything he said.

"We need to identify everyone in the building who had contact with our Indonesian doctor," Dr Cromwell began. "They should be put on antivirals, the sooner the better." He glared at Michael, as if this were all his fault.

"For the flu?" Dr Stratford asked. "Most of them had flu shots. All my people did. I don't understand what all this fuss is about."

"Yes, what is this about?" Valarie asked.

Michael spoke up. "I got an email a couple of days ago from Dr Gordon, over at the health department? She said that the World Health Organization was investigating an outbreak of a new strain of flu in Indonesia."

"Is that the bird flu?" Valarie asked.

"Yes, it is a bird flu," Dr Cromwell said. "But not the bird flu that has been in the news. This one is an H7. H7N1. Highly pathogenic in birds. Apparently in humans, too. The World Health Organization has been trying to verify person-to-person spread." Dr Cromwell looked around for something to drink. It used to be that a carafe of iced water and glasses were placed around the conference table during meetings. And coffee brewing on a table at the back of the room. This was just not civilized.

Cromwell cleared his throat and continued. "There have been a lot of reports coming out of Indonesia of hospitals full of patients with virulent pneumonia and influenza A. Very little of it is official though. The clinical picture is similar to the H5N1 cases they've had. High mortality. But the H5N1 testing has all come back negative. Some lab in Norway identified it as H7N1, they reported it just yesterday on Pro-MED. Now there is a lot of hullabaloo from Indonesia about how the Norwegians got the specimen in the first place." He realized he was getting off-track, but he loved having an audience. "At any rate, that's the concern. Indonesia appears to be having an outbreak of a highly virulent, novel flu strain, with person-to-person spread."

"The hallmark of a new flu pandemic," Michael chimed in. He pushed his glasses up on his nose, making Dr Cromwell cringe.

"And one of their physicians is in our hospital?" the safety officer asked.

"Yes," Dr Cromwell said. He paused for dramatic effect. "A physician who works in a teaching hospital in Jakarta is sick with the flu and is lying in our ICU."

"I don't understand," piped up Valarie. "Didn't the lab run some tests on him? Doesn't he have influenza A? How do you know it is not just regular flu?"

Donna shivered and pulled her sweater tighter around her body and answered. "H7N1 is a type of influenza A. Our tests can only identify if a person has influenza A or B. It can't distinguish what strain of flu the person has." She turned and looked at Michael. "We need to get specimens to the state lab to verify H7N1. I don't even know if they can do that. They can test for H5N1, but I doubt they have the primers for this H7N1 strain yet. It may have to go to Atlanta. To the CDC. Mike, can you arrange for that to happen through the health department?"

"Does Dr Gordon even know about this yet?" Dr Stratford asked.

"I need to call her. I'll get the lab situation arranged, find out what all they need from us. She doesn't know yet. I wanted us to all meet first," Michael said.

The risk manager sighed loudly. "Once the health department gets wind of this, things are going to get really busy around here. We should go into incident command now, open the emergency operations center. Where the hell is the public information officer? Why isn't she here? No one leak this to the media, please. We don't need them poking around until we are sure everything is under control. Please, people."

They all looked at Dr Cromwell. While technically not in charge, he had an air of authority about him. "Let's do it then," he said.

Julia fiddled with her iPhone under the table. Eliza watched her; she appeared to be playing a video game.

"So what do you think, Julia?" Eliza asked. She knew that Julia had no idea what she was talking about. She had called this meeting a week ago when the new guidelines for control of staph skin infections among school athletes were released from the state health department. She asked everyone to familiarize themselves with them so they could brainstorm about how to best go about implementation.

"Oh, I, um, well, I am not sure."

"You have no opinion about the section on locker rooms, or about the guidelines at all? You did read them, right?" Eliza asked. Geoff snickered. He jumped in to rescue her.

"I think the intent is good," he said, "but I think there will be some problems with implementation."

"Yeah, definitely," Julia agreed. She put her iPhone up on the conference table.

"What problems do you see, Julia?" asked Eliza. She wasn't going to let this one go. It was her passive-aggressive attempt at control. She couldn't stand having such a worthless employee supposedly working for her. Julia worked on the mayoral campaign as part of the Young Republicans at the university last year, and he gave her this job after he got elected. Eliza had no respect for people appointed to high-level positions just because they kissed some ass. That, and Eliza voted Democrat. The worst part, though, was that she couldn't fire Julia. Not unless Julia did something hideous, something law-breaking. Julia could be a substandard government employee as long as she wanted. Conceivably, Eliza could get rid of her if a Democrat was elected mayor, but Dalton's super-conservative electorate would probably not ever let that happen. She'd be stuck with Julia until retirement.

Julia did not respond. Her face turned red. She looked down at her paper.

Lucy poked her head into the conference room. "Dr E, Michael from Memorial Hospital is on the phone for you. I am sorry to interrupt, but he said it was important."

Eliza resented the interruption, but the meeting was going nowhere anyway. She stood up and walked toward the door. "Lucy, please reschedule this meeting for next week. See what fits into my calendar." She looked back at Julia. "Will everyone please read the recommendations and have constructive input next time? Thank you." Frustrated, she walked out of the room and went to her office.

"Michael, how are you, my friend?" she asked.

"Hey, Dr E. I've got something big. I apologize in advance."

"Michael, is this going to be one of those days where I go home and have to open a bottle of wine?"

"I'm afraid so. Yesterday a guy was brought to our ER by ambulance in respiratory distress. High fever. Delirious. They intubated him."

"Bacterial meningitis?" she asked.

"Good guess, but nope. They gave him a spinal tap. The cerebral spinal fluid was clear, no sign of bacterial meningitis. But he did get back a rapid test positive for flu."

"Flu? Ok."

"Hang on, this gets good. His wife shows up, drives herself in a rental car behind the ambulance. Her English is terrible. Takes us forever to get someone to help translate. Turns out they are from Indonesia, here for a conference."

"Indonesia, really?" Eliza leaned back in her chair. "Now this is getting interesting."

"Yeah, and he's a doc. Hospitalist."

"Awesome." Eliza could feel the hairs on her arms stand at attention. "So are you thinking it's bird flu?" She lived for cases like this.

"You got it," Michael said.

She stood up; she always stood up when she was excited about a case. "I am going to fax you over a reporting form. Warning you in advance, it is really long. I need you to send me all of his demographics, a copy of his history and physical, and all of the consultation notes."

"Most of that is not electronic yet. Do you want the originals?"

"Is it one of Cromwell's patients?"

"Yeah."

"No. I won't be able to read any of it," she said. Cromwell's handwriting was terrible. She thought it was a miracle that it could be transcribed at all. "Fax it as soon as it is in the system. See if Cromwell can get someone to transcribe it now."

"Will do. Can you help us with the lab work?"

"Of course. I'll have to call the state and arrange for your specimens to be sent there. Don't collect anything else until I get back to you on that and be sure they hold on to everything they've already got, especially that spinal fluid. You do have him in isolation, right?"

"Yeah, but we have some exposures. Cromwell's already ordered antivirals for all of them."

"And the wife?"

"She's here. We'll take care of her too."

"I need someone to find out what flights he was on and where they were staying. The CDC quarantine folks can pull the manifests, but I've got to have his flight numbers. Your translator still around?"

"Yeah, we found a woman in housekeeping who can do it."

"All the questions are on the reporting form, I'm faxing it over. I need this back ASAP. She's gonna need a bonus after this. Tell Cromwell to get her one."

Michael laughed. "Because of his large humanitarian heart? Don't hold your breath. Anything else?"

"Not that I can think of, but you know I will be calling you soon with more. I'll get back to you after I talk with the state."

"Thanks, Dr E. When this is done I'll buy ya a margarita."

"I'm going to hold you to that, Michael."

The priest sat in his car in front of Cassandra's house, debating what to say to her, how best to approach her. He knew all about the services she provided to the community and while he technically had to condemn her practices, he could hardly deny them. He secretly believed she was gifted. He'd seen the results of her healing in his congregation. Women whose doctors had declared to be infertile became pregnant after a visit with her. She seemed to have a special knack for asthma. After children with asthma saw Cassandra, they didn't need to have medication or breathing treatments anymore. She even cured José Riviera's diabetes; José said his doctor was thrilled with his blood sugar counts. His cholesterol went down too. And frankly, though this was not supposed to be of interest for him either, the priest found her quite beautiful.

His visit today was on false pretenses. He planned to apologize for their argument and invite her back to Mass. He hoped, though, that she could rid him of his cough.

Cassandra dug through the ground near the back fence, pulling up sweet onions. A grey and white cat rubbed up against her.

"You pesky little thing. Onions are not for cats." She reached out and scratched him behind the ears.

"Excuse me. Cassandra?"

Cassandra yelped. The cat jumped, its tail in a puff, and scampered under the fence.

"Mary Mother of God, you startled me, Father!" The sight of the priest in the yard intrigued her, yet it felt right having this holy man in her sacred space. She had to remind herself that she was angry with him.

"I am terribly sorry, I didn't mean to, I just wanted…" the priest stumbled through his words.

"Father Kreston, it is alright. I am happy to have you as a guest at my home." She stood up, brushing the dirt off of her hands.

"I wanted to speak with you." He coughed a couple of times into his hand. "About returning to Mass." He coughed several times uncontrollably.

She laughed to herself and picked up the basket of onions. "Come inside, Father." She winked at him. "Perhaps we can pray together."

He nodded, trying to stifle his cough. He hated how his body always betrayed him.

Inside she set the onions on one of the kitchen counters. "Do you cook? You can have some of these if you want. They are wonderful."

"Yes, actually, I do." He began coughing again. "Do you have? A glass?" She gestured toward the cabinet. As he drew himself a glass of water he daydreamed about cooking for her.

She pulled a large glass jar from the shelf. It held bundles of pale furry leaves tied together with twine.

"I came to invite you back to church, Cassandra. Everyone misses you."

"Did you also come to apologize?"

"Yes, I did, in fact. I apologize for making you feel unwelcome. I apologize for hurting you." He wanted to reach out to her, to tuck the lock of hair that had fallen in front of her eyes behind her ear. To take her in his arms.

"And do you apologize for calling me a witch? Let's see, what was it? A dark sorceress?"

That embarrassed him. Too much wine and he had gone overboard with his proselytizing.

She took a box of red-tipped matches out of one of the drawers and lit the herbs on fire. Her lips in a kiss, she blew on them until they smoldered and placed them in a hammered copper bowl sitting in the center of the kitchen table. She draped a coil of ebony rosary beads over the side of the bowl. Jesus watched him from the tiny cross. Wisps of smoke wafted across the room. Father Kreston fought his growing erection, and cursed his body for the second time that day for its betrayal.

"You know there are certain principles I must uphold," he said. "But I admit, I was too forceful, too..." His words drifted off. He could feel the smoke opening his airways. He inhaled deeply and looked into her dark almond eyes and knew she could see into the blackness of his soul.

"Thank you, Cassandra," he said, breathing easily.

"You are always welcome, Father."

Eliza read Michael's email again. It was to the point: Dr Sitala is dead. *Who the hell is Dr Sitala?*

"Michael, what is this?" she asked when he answered the phone.

"He's our patient. The Indonesian doctor? Sorry, I should have given you his name before. We lost him just a little while ago."

"Damn it. You tell the lab to guard those specimens. Fort Knox. Damn. What did they get?"

"Don't worry. We've got blood, urine, and the CSF. Cromwell even went ahead and got sputum and a bronchial wash."

"Bless that crazy man. Did he do the procedure himself?"

"Yeah, him and a pulmonologist. They didn't want to wait to hear back from you and the state lab. They were in PAPRs."

Eliza was glad to hear that. The powered air purifying respirators covered the entire head and neck and had their own filtered air intake system to keep the health care worker from getting splashed in the face with virus during the procedure. There was some evidence during the SARS outbreak that the coronavirus particles were so small that they could enter the body through the eyes. It was unlikely that this influenza virus was that small; flu viruses tended to be larger. Regular flu was anyway. Better to go overboard on safety though, especially since they did not know exactly what they were dealing with.

"Tell me that the wife is amenable to autopsy."

"Fortunately, yes."

"Well, yea for that."

"About the wife. We just admitted her too. She's in isolation with a cough. She went down crazy fast. One minute she's fine, the next she is really sick."

"You're kidding."

"I'm afraid not. I'll get you paperwork on her too."

"Tell Donna to go ahead and collect specimens on the wife too."

"She's on it."

"You'll love this. The state health department wants us to fly the specimens to their lab. I need you to talk with your facilities people. They are sending a state trooper helicopter, they want to land on your helipad. Donna needs to meet them. She'll have to sign a chain of custody form." Eliza tangled the phone cord around her fingers and wished she could fly on the helicopter too. That would make a great story for Sophie.

Eliza glanced up at the clock on the wall. She should have gone home thirty minutes ago. Tonight will be a long night, she thought.

She didn't want to call Steven. While he always pretended to be sweet and understanding about her job, she knew he hated when she had to work late, and when she heard it in his voice she felt guilty. Worse, he would put Sophie on the phone – *say hello to Mommy, we won't see her tonight* – really ratcheting up the guilt meter. She decided to email him instead and call him later.

She drew out an organizational chart on the conference room white board. They had to fill in a chart for every emergency. Ever since 9/11, all emergency response organizations had to, it was part of the National Incident Management System. The feds tied all the emergency preparedness funding to it, made them all sit through hours and hours of tedious classes on how to talk to each other during an emergency. She thought this qualified as an emergency. She put herself down as the Intelligence Chief. She did not want to be stuck as Incident Commander, even though her boss usually pushed her to do it. The Incident Commander had to coordinate everything. That person got all the glory, but she wanted to be part of the action, not head of the bureaucracy. Her colleagues filtered into the room.

"Dr E, do you want me to set up the Star Trek phone?" Lucy asked.

"Yes, we'll need it."

The Star Trek phone (so they called it) was a grey, triangular-shaped console used for making conference calls. It flashed with green lights when active, red lights when muted. It sat at the center of the round conference table and allowed everyone to participate in the call. It was important to note what color light was flashing before speaking; many a faux pas was made on the assumption that the thing was muted.

"Who's taking command?" Geoff asked. He looked at Eliza.

"Forget it. We are doing intel. Jack's the Incident Commander."

At that, Jack walked into the room. "I'm in charge? Great!" He winked at her and sat at the head of the table. Jack flirted with all of the women he encountered. Everyone said that he could have his pick of middle-aged school nurses. They all loved him. In truth, Jack was gay, but few of his colleagues knew that. A short man, he

17

dressed in expensive suits and colorful ties, and used his prematurely gray hair to his advantage; most people assumed he was older than he really was.

The emergency manager from the police department sat down next to him. He looked like a SWAT team member, dressed in a tight black shirt, black pants, black boots, gun on his hip. Eliza always appreciated his presence at her meetings. He was very nice to look at.

"Dr E, I've got a line open," Lucy said. "Does anyone want some coffee? I can brew some." Several people nodded.

"So Eliza, why have you dragged us all over here today?" the emergency manager asked.

"Let's wait until everyone is on the line. Catch us all up at once," Jack said.

A loud beep emanated from the phone. "Hello? Anyone here yet?" A voice asked.

"Hello Michael, this is Dr Gordon. We'll do role call in a minute." Eliza hated the confusion of the first few minutes of a conference call, while everyone ensured that yes, they were in fact on the line. The phone beeped several more times, all with scattered greetings. Finally she decided to begin.

"Let's get started. This is Dr Eliza Gordon, Chief Epidemiologist with the Dalton Public Health Department. I have with me the Health Department Director and our Health Authority; Jack Karl, our Public Health Preparedness Director; Grant Maguire, the city Emergency Manager; the city Public Information Officer; and several people from the epidemiology and the preparedness departments. Jack Karl is the Incident Commander. I am the Intelligence Chief. Memorial, are you on?"

"This is Michael Kzyski, Infection Control Director at Dalton Memorial Hospital. I have Dr Benjamin Cromwell, our infectious disease physician, Donna Pascoe, our microbiologist, and Sarah McWhorter, our Chief Nursing Officer here with me."

"Is anyone on from the state health department?" Eliza asked.

"This is Richard Reeves, State Epidemiologist for the state of Texas. I have several of my team members with me."

"Jan Rainy, State of Texas lab director, and Chad Marshal, from virology."

"Thanks for joining us. CDC?"

"CDC Office of Quarantine on the line."

"CDC virus labs."

"This is George Garland, I am with the CDC Influenza Division. Jack McMillon from the Strategic National Stockpile is here with me."

"It is nice to have all of you here. Thanks for joining us. Anyone else on?" Eliza took a sip from the cup of coffee Lucy sat in front of her.

"We'll try to keep this call brief, I know we all have lots to do. Memorial, would you like to start?" Jack said.

"Sure. Yesterday morning a physician from Indonesia was transported to our ER in respiratory distress. He was intubated. The ER docs did a spinal tap and ran some rapid tests. He was positive for influenza A."

"What other tests did you do?" someone asked.

"We did strep, it was negative. No growth as of yet on the blood and CSF cultures. CSF was clear. He's leucopenic. Chest x-ray showed consolidation of his right lung. Once he stabilized, we admitted him to the ICU," Michael said.

"Fortunately, they called me in pretty quick," Dr Cromwell said. "Indonesian doctor, red flag. I had him put in airborne isolation and required everyone to take appropriate precautions. We did have a lot of exposures early on though, in the ER and in the lab. The patient seized in the ambulance, so we had some exposures there. We've got everyone on antivirals. We had to call a couple of hospitals in our system to get enough drugs for everyone. We do not have a stockpile of antivirals here, despite my repeated requests that we do so."

"The patient's wife was with him," Michael said. "We kept her in isolation as a precaution. She became symptomatic this afternoon. We went ahead and admitted her."

"The doctor died not long ago. His wife has agreed to an autopsy," Cromwell said.

"This is CDC. We want the body."

"I don't see a problem with that," Dr Cromwell said. "The wife was very cooperative. She understands the situation. Dr Sitala – the patient – he was a hospitalist in Jakarta. She said he had treated some of the pneumonia patients there, the H7N1 patients. She said he had met with the World Health Organization on it, and he's been involved in some of their influenza research. He had been scheduled to present some of his work at a conference at the university in town this week."

"When did they get to the US?" someone asked.

"Day before yesterday. They flew in to San Antonio, drove in to Dalton. They went out to dinner that night at a local Italian place, checked in to the Marriot. Didn't leave again until the 911 call," Michael said.

"When was his onset of symptoms?"

"On the plane, a couple of hours after he left. Told his wife he felt feverish, had a bit of a cough."

"And he was dead two days later?" the emergency manager asked.

"Three, actually, once you account for travel time. This is the CDC Office of Quarantine. Dr Gordon gave us the flight numbers and we have been in contact with the airlines. We still don't have the manifests, but we should have them soon. We have also been in contact with WHO and the Indonesian Ministry of Health. WHO verified that Dr Sitala has been working with H7N1 patients. The good doctor took off from Jakarta and landed in Tokyo, where he had a three-hour layover. Next he was off to Honolulu. Four hours waiting there, then a flight to Los Angeles. Two hours in LA and then on in to San Antonio."

"Cripes, was that a long trip. We're talking hundreds of opportunities for exposure," someone said.

"This is the first I have heard about San Antonio. Does anyone know about other exposures there? Did they get something to eat? Gas? I'll alert the San Antonio Health Department," the State Epidemiologist said.

"This is CDC. Texas, do you want to make a formal request for the Strategic National Stockpile now?"

"I can only do it unofficially on this call, but yes, you should prepare for it," the State Epi answered. "It will have to go through the proper channels. We may have enough antiviral drugs to give to everyone who has been exposed, we do have a stockpile, but if we don't have enough, I don't want them to be delayed."

"Once we get the official request, we can get the stockpile to the San Antonio health department in under six hours. There is a cache not far away."

Eliza had always assumed there were drugs and supplies positioned in Texas in case of a public health emergency just based on population size, but the location was kept confidential. The emergency manager jumped in. "I understand from DPS they have a helicopter en route to pick up some lab work?"

"Yes," Eliza said. "They will be taking the specimens back to the lab at the state health department. While all of the epidemiology points to Dr Sitala being infected with H7N1, we want the lab to confirm that."

"What if he wasn't?"

"Then we will all stand down. Tell the folks at Memorial they can stop taking the meds and breathe easy. And we can take Mrs Sitala out of isolation," Jack said.

"Is there anything else we need to discuss at this point?" the health department director asked.

"Yes. This is George Garland from CDC Influenza Division. This hasn't been made public yet, but the World Health Organization intends to announce that they have confirmed person-to-person spread of H7N1. There are literally hundreds of cases in Indonesia. There's been some suggestion in Pro-MED that it is all concentrated in Jakarta, but that's not really true. They have a lot of cases there, but it is really in the villages, where people have very little access to health care services. They are in a state of emergency. We are looking at a mortality rate of nearly 45 percent. We had planned to put out a travel advisory first thing tomorrow morning. The lawyers are going over it now. I can put up an Epi-X on your case tonight if you want me to."

"An Epi-X?" asked the emergency manager.

"That's our epidemic information exchange network. Epidemiologists all over the country have access to it. It is a secure system, they have to have security clearance to access it. Honolulu, LA, San Antonio... We know the patient spent time in each. There's no telling who he had contact with. People traveling, traveling all over the US, all over the world for that matter. This will let all the epis know what's going on, and to keep an eye out for more cases," Garland said.

"Once we get the flight manifests, we will alert the local health departments of every US citizen on those planes," the quarantine official said. "We give them a script they use to call the passengers and see if they have symptoms, advise them what to do if they are symptomatic, and tell them what to do if they start developing symptoms. We do this all the time with TB, measles, rubella, and whatnot, so the process is pretty streamlined."

"The most important thing is for everyone to start looking for possible cases and *get them isolated*. We've got to minimize any spread," Dr Garland said. "Dalton, you may have the dubious honor of having the index patient for the next influenza pandemic."

CHAPTER 2

Dalton, Texas
Total infected = 7
Total dead = 1

God, I hate paperwork, Donna thought. Bent over her desk, she shuffled through forms. *And damn, why is it so freaking cold in here?* She pulled on her sweater but still shivered. She decided to get out of her office for a while.

The lab was quiet. Everyone had gone to lunch. Donna picked up a vial of blood out of the drop box. It must have just been drawn; the tube felt warm. She looked for the request form. The physician had ordered a complete blood count, a routine test that looked at a patient's overall health status. She'd run hundreds of CBCs. She placed the vial inside a large machine, flipped on a switch, and waited. She didn't mind doing blood; in fact, she found it interesting, identifying organisms in people's blood. Stool samples grossed her out. And vomit. Sometimes she had to do tests on vomit. That was disgusting, opening a container of fresh vomit, removing a sample for analysis. As the lab director, though, she could usually delegate that to one of the lab techs and just peek in on the final results. Since they promoted her to director, though, she didn't have to do much of any actual lab work anymore. Now she was an administrator. With her paperwork. But this CBC, she would do this.

The cough started with a tickle at the back of her throat. Pressure in her sinuses. Allergies, she thought. She coughed into the crook of her arm, trying not to contaminate her hands. When the machine finished, she entered the results into the patient's electronic medical record. The physician would have the results immediately.

She left the lab for the cafeteria. Along the way she decided she worked much too hard. She felt exhausted.

"Donna!" Someone called her name. She turned to see Michael walking towards her.

"Mind if I join you for lunch?" he asked.

"Sure," she said.

"So I was in a meeting this morning, you know, one of those God-awful meetings to nowhere that drag on and on, the physicians all referring to themselves as Doctor this and Doctor that, and trying to out-pompous each other? Dr Cromwell bragging about catching that H7N1 patient – the state confirmed it, did you know? Then Dr Pierce, from cardiology? He absolutely blasts Dr Cromwell for the bronchial wash, said it was medically unnecessary, and that Cromwell jeopardized the patient's well-being and put himself and his team at risk, berates him on the infection control issue. And everyone starts agreeing with him! It was great! Cromwell got all huffed up, face turned red, red! Stands up, yelling, defending himself, and then Pierce gets up too. Cromwell's pointing his finger at Pierce, citing his credentials and Pierce is practically jumping over the table, questioning Cromwell's ethics, and citing research at him, we're talking journal articles with their authors and everything. Cromwell gets all kinds of worked up, spit flying from his mouth, and Valarie, of all people, Valarie says, 'Dr Cromwell, please calm down, your saliva is going to cause an infection control issue in here.' She got a huge laugh. He looked like such a dumbass."

"Huh," said Donna. She poured herself a bowl of soup and threw several packets of crackers on her tray.

"Isn't that great?" Michael said.

"That is. Wild."

"Are you ok, Donna? You look pale."

She closed her eyes and inhaled deeply. "I'm sorry, Michael. I'm afraid I am not very good company today. Honestly, I feel like I have been run over by a truck."

He looked closely at her. "Have you seen anyone about it?"

"Naw, I'll be fine. I don't think I am getting enough rest, that's all. I'll be fine." She placed her hand on her abdomen for a moment. *Morning sickness*, she thought. She smiled weakly at him, still not ready to share news of her pregnancy. She wanted to get to the second trimester first, just to be sure.

Michael grabbed a turkey sandwich on whole wheat bread and a small salad. "It's not like there aren't any doctors around to help you."

Donna paid for her lunch and looked around the cafeteria for an open table. "Maybe I'll go later," she said.

"You know they live for that," Michael said. "Make's them feel like God."

Dr Cromwell sat in his car in the hospital parking lot, near the spots designated for labor and delivery patients. He watched the pregnant women as they got out of their cars, grabbing their bellies, usually, but not always, accompanied by a frightened-looking man. One woman's pants were drenched from the crotch down in amniotic fluid. Every few steps, she stopped, grimaced, and beared down. *She's going to go right here in the parking lot*, he thought. *Please, show some dignity woman.* But, no, she made her way up the steps and into the building.

Cromwell didn't attend the births of his children. Back then, that was unheard of. No, the man's place was in the waiting room with a handful of cigars.

He'd been married twice. Neither marriage worked out. His wives couldn't compete with infectious diseases – they were vastly more interesting than any woman he'd ever met. His wives happily spent all his money while constantly complaining about the long hours it took to make that money. His two sons, they were from his first wife. What disappointments they turned out to be. The one went to college for a degree in theater, of all things. Because that would land him a good job. Cromwell didn't even know a person could get a degree in theater when the boy signed up. The boy graduated and now waited tables in New York. Waited for his talent to be discovered. Been waiting for quite some time now. The other one majored in business. He works as a middle manager in a department store. A nice way of saying that his son worked at the mall. That one married a trashy girl with lots of tattoos a few years ago. Shotgun wedding. The wife gave birth six months later. Had another one in less than a year. He carried pictures of the grandkids in his wallet and sometimes thought about getting to know them better, but he didn't have much contact. He rarely saw either of his sons, but he did make a point of sending them both a check at Christmas. Which they each promptly cashed without as much as a thank you.

The second wife wanted to have kids but she was barren, a blessing in his eyes. She would have adopted, but he had no interest in that. Neither marriage ended pleasantly, big mess both times. Cost him a fortune, those women. And they both hated him to this day. He glanced up at the signs designating labor and delivery parking. They were decorated with cutesy storks. No, marriage was a mistake.

He flipped through the journal article in his lap. The words danced on the page in front of him. A rarity, but today he had no interest in the nuts and bolts of viruses, bacteria, all of that. This Indonesian flu worried him. The sun filtered through the tree leaves and filled his car with shadows of irregular shape. He started the engine, put the car in gear, and decided to take Dr Gordon to lunch.

"Any way that you could help, please, they will fire me at the restaurant if I miss work." Juan sat down at Cassandra's kitchen table.

"Aye, you hate that job anyway," teased his wife. "Big strong man, washing the white people's dishes while his wife stays at home watching the white people's children. Who would have thought this would be our lives? Doing white people's chores. We are slaves."

Cassandra burned herbs over Juan's head and said a prayer. Normally she laughed at his wife's antics, but his rapid breathing and the sound of his inhalations alarmed her. His lungs crackled audibly with each breath. His nostrils flared with the effort. A thin tinge of dusty blue outlined his lips.

"Juan, I think you need to go to the hospital," she said.

Juan's face filled with surprise. He had known Cassandra for years. She seldom dealt with the Western medical community.

"It's that bad?" he asked, but he knew the answer, knew he needed to be at the hospital. A million needles stabbed him at every gulp of air.

"It's that bad."

His wife hugged her. "Thank you, Cassandra. We will go. Give this man some time to rest. Give those vampires our pennies." She chuckled, but a worried look flashed across her face. A paroxysm of coughing wracked Juan's body. When the coughing finally stopped, he held up his hands, covered in blood-tinged mucus. "Jesus," he whispered.

"Let us go now," Juan's wife said. "Cassandra, we will call you, yes?"

"Please." She continued to pray as they walked out the door. She cleaned the kitchen with a solution of bleach and water, poured herself a glass of wine, and hoped that she had not just contracted tuberculosis.

"Dr E, there is someone here to see you," Lucy said on the phone.

"Who is it?" She checked her calendar. "I don't have an appointment."

"A Mr Benjamin Cromwell."

"Dr Cromwell? I'll be right there." Eliza had worked with Dr Cromwell for years, but always over the phone. It occurred to her that she had never actually met him in person. She fluffed up her hair and walked into the lobby.

"Dr Gordon?" Dr Cromwell reached out his hand to shake hers.

"Please, call me Eliza," she said.

He smiled at her, his pale blue eyes crinkling at the corners. His white hair and pot belly reminded her of a Norman Rockwell grandfather. Or Santa Claus. "Only if you call me Ben," he said.

"What can I do for you today, Ben?" He had always been Cromwell; Ben tripped her tongue.

"You can give me the pleasure of taking you out to lunch."

"To lunch?" She realized he was flirting with her. She flirted back. "How long have we known each other, Dr....Ben? You have never invited me to lunch before. What is this about?"

"I know. How terrible of me. You must think me exceedingly rude. Do you like Thai food?"

"I do."

"Then collect your things. I know a great Thai place."

Lunch patrons swarmed the Siam Palace. Dr Cromwell appeared to be a regular though; a table waited for him in the corner.

"Have you been here before? The chicken with sweet basil is excellent."

"Once," she said. "I think I had the pad Thai." She scanned the menu.

"Ah, another good selection. Tell me, what do you think of our H7N1 fellow?"

"What do you mean?"

"Do you think, speaking as a professional epidemiologist, do you think that we are on the brink of catastrophe?"

She laughed. "That seems a bit sensationalistic, don't you think?" She took a sip of water. "It was one case. Well, two cases, with the wife. Michael said everyone at the hospital took precautions, and those who didn't early on were put on antivirals."

"Michael is an idiot. You shouldn't believe a word he says," Dr Cromwell said. He nodded to the waiter and ordered chicken with sweet basil and hot jasmine tea for both of them. "Do you want spring rolls?" he asked. He ordered some before she could respond. She handed her clearly unneeded menu back to the waiter.

"Now, where were we? Ah, yes! Catastrophe. Have you ever read any of the manuscripts on the influenza pandemic of 1918?"

"Of course. It's a great study on how modern medicine, if you want to call 1918 modern, coped with a large-scale infectious disease outbreak."

"And in 1918, do you agree, it was a catastrophe? Millions of people around the world dead. Comparable to the Black Plague?"

"Yes, lots of dead, although there's been some debate on that point, particularly in regards to how the deaths were recorded, if they were all really influenza or if other causes of death were mixed in with them. Proportionally, though, the Black Plague wrecked more havoc ..."

He cut her off. "I think that we are on the cusp, the cusp, of such another tragedy today. And we, Eliza, we are not ready for it. Memorial certainly cannot cope with anything on scale with the 1918 pandemic. Hundreds, maybe even thousands of people at our doors? We can't do it. We run at ninety-eight percent capacity under normal conditions. There are no extra beds. During regular influenza season we've been known to run out of beds. Not to mention the fact that we have a critical shortage of nurses at any given moment. No. We are not prepared for this."

Eliza realized she had never known Dr Cromwell to be dramatic. Generally, he was very business-like with her, short, to the point. But then, much of her understanding of him had been filtered through Michael. That Michael and Dr Cromwell hated each other was common knowledge.

"Well. Then. Here's our food. Quick. Quick service here. One thing I like about this place." He picked up some chopsticks and began to eat.

"Well, as far as being prepared, I think ..." Eliza began.

"Oh no, please." Dr Cromwell cut her off again. "I never discuss business while eating."

She tried, but could not get him back on the catastrophe topic. She gave up and showed him pictures of Sophie. He showed her pictures of his grandchildren in return.

Geoff poked his head into Eliza's office doorway. "Hey, Dr E. The chancellor from the university is on the line. He wants to speak with you."

"Ok, transfer him over to me." She saved the edits of her H7N1 report. Several of the CDC people wanted her to write up what happened for a journal article with them.

She picked up the phone. "Hello? This is Dr Gordon."

"Dr Gordon, thank you for taking my call. We have a situation over here. Did your assistant tell you, or will I have to explain myself again?" The chancellor sounded angry.

"I apologize, but he did not fill me in. What can I help you with?"

"I am calling to find out the status of a Dr Sitala. Our biology department invited him to be the keynote speaker at their conference this week, and he is not here. I understand you may know of his whereabouts?"

Confidentiality issues were sometimes tricky. The health department could only release information when people had been exposed to a communicable disease. If no exposure occurred, patient's privacy had to be protected. "I'm sorry. I cannot give you any information. That is covered by privacy laws."

"Is your job not disease control?" the chancellor asked.

"Yes, it is."

"Then are you not responsible for disease control on my campus?"

"I have no reason to believe that your campus is at risk of any disease exposure from that patient. As such, I cannot release any information to you."

"Dr Gordon, perhaps you are not aware – perhaps I should give you the benefit of the doubt – because I just became aware of this issue this morning. Several of my biology faculty members took Dr Sitala and his wife to dinner when they arrived in town. One then hosted after-dinner cocktails in her home. Of course, when he did not show the next day for their conference, their speaker whom they had flown in from Indonesia at a significant expense, they scrambled to locate him. Finally, one of them spoke with Mrs Sitala on the phone yesterday; Mrs Sitala called the university from the hospital. She said that Dr Sitala died suddenly, and that it was believed by your office that he was infected with a novel strain of influenza virus, one that is highly lethal. And now I have two faculty members who are reporting that they are ill. Now tell me, Dr Gordon, how is that not of your concern?"

Eliza took a deep breath to calm herself. She wanted to explode at the chancellor. "Sir, Mrs Sitala did not inform us that she went to dinner with, nor to the home of, any of your faculty members. Had I known, I can assure you we would have performed the appropriate disease control measures."

"Shouldn't you have checked a little further into this? Do you know the potential I have here for media hoopla? Not to mention liability?"

"Well, let's try to avoid that. I need a list of all of the faculty members who were around the Sitalas, and contact information for them. We will follow up with them directly to discuss any disease control measures."

"So what of Dr Sitala, is he in fact dead from a new flu strain?"

She decided to verify what the chancellor already knew. "Yes. He is."

"I see."

Eliza did not respond. The chancellor continued. "I will have someone from biology call you with all of the information. You should know that the two who are sick have been on campus and have been teaching classes."

"Ok. The typical protocol is for us to work through your student health center. Would you like for us to do that in this case?"

"Yes. By all means follow the protocol. But please copy me on any emails. I will inform the health center that they should be expecting to hear from you soon. I would like to be kept apprised of the situation."

She hung up the phone and looked up the phone number for the biology department on the Internet. She would not wait for them to call her. A new Pro-MED report popped up in her email. In it, she read a report from Los Angeles of suspected H7N1 cases in two of their hospitals. *On the cusp of tragedy, indeed.*

CHAPTER 3

Dr Cromwell listened to Donna's chest.

"Deep breath," he said. She tried to comply. She felt like she had a vice-grip on her lungs, locked down tight. It hurt to breath.

"It's H7N1, I know it is," she said.

He looked at her, his eyebrows raised. "What makes you say that? You're on antivirals."

She glanced away from his gaze. "I can't take them," she said. "I'm pregnant."

Cromwell sighed and pinched the bridge of his nose. "Donna, if you are coming to me for care, I need to be aware of things like that. How far along are you?"

"Just a few weeks."

"Did you take any of the medication?"

"No. It's contraindicated in pregnancy. I tested myself for flu. It was positive. I'm telling you, I've got it."

"Again, information you should have shared with me before you asked me to listen to your chest. I'm going to order an X-ray for you."

"The baby. I can't have an X-ray."

"You can, we can cover your abdomen – "

"No. I mean, I won't."

"Donna, please." He placed his hand on her shoulder. "Your lungs sound bad. I promise I will do everything in my power to protect your baby. We'll shoot one x-ray, just one, and we'll wrap your abdomen in a lead blanket. I need to know what we're dealing with. I need to know, so I can save both of you."

Donna started to cry.

"I'll talk to Dr Russels over in obstetrics, we'll bring him in as well. Okay?" he said. She nodded.

Cromwell went to order the portable X-ray machine. Bad news for Donna, although she should have spoken up sooner. All of the reports coming out of Indonesia on pregnant women with this virus had bad outcomes. H7N1 crossed the placenta. He had yet to hear of a case when either patient, mom or baby, survived. If she did, he would write it up. Surely he could get a publication out of all of this.

Radiology had the film back quickly; people around the hospital moved faster when it was one of their own. At least they did if it was someone they liked. "I want to admit you," Dr Cromwell said. He stood in front of a large light panel, blackened out with an X-ray of Donna's fluid-filled lungs. The mask on his face muffled his voice. He spared her another exposure lecture. Donna had already heard it from Michael and from the Chief Nursing Officer, how her sloppy protocols had put her and the hospital staff at risk. How this had all become her fault. Michael added more healthcare workers to his list of people on antiviral medications. The entire lab had been exposed to her coughing and to culture plates of Dr Sitala's secretions left out to grow. Michael yelled at her for that. And she saw the fear in his eyes. The fear, that hurt her more than the yelling. The fear that mirrored her own. She exposed him, too.

But right now she didn't care. Her head sunk back into the pillow. She couldn't hold it up any longer. An IV pole stood at attention at her side, its snake-like tubing coiled against her arm, a long, slender fang pierced into the soft flesh at the crook of her elbow, rehydrating her parched body. Dr Cromwell typed an order for medications into his PDA, which transmitted directly to the hospital pharmacy.

One of her lab technicians entered the room, carrying a tray filled with phlebotomy supplies. The tech had a pale green paper gown tied on over her scrubs, latex gloves on her hands, an N95 mask covered her face. Air rushed into the room when the door opened; Donna lay in an isolation room. Signs on the door warned the healthcare workers to don proper protective gear before entering. That really made her feel contaminated. Dirty. Dr Cromwell put her in here when she admitted it to him, while he examined her, her breech in protocols in the lab with Dr Sitala's specimens. "Honestly," Donna said through tears, "I thought it was just the flu."

Her stomach cramped and lurched. Vomit spewed across her lap.

"Jesus." Cromwell rushed over to her as she choked and gasped for air. Her body thrashed on the bed in a seizure, her eyes rolled around in their sockets. The IV ripped out of her flailing arm. Dr Cromwell cursed the nurse who inserted the needle and didn't secure it better with tape. "Get someone!" he yelled at the tech. She ran out into the hallway, ripping off her mask, screaming at the nurses' station for help.

Dr Cromwell held Donna's head back, forced her throat open. He jammed one of his fingers into her mouth, holding her tongue and blocking her teeth from chewing up her cheeks. "Hang with me, Donna!"

Through the glass door he watched the crash team worming into their protective gear. A nurse burst into the room. "Dr?"

"I'll hold her. You get another IV started."

The pulmonologist and another nurse followed. "She's crashing!" Cromwell yelled at them. Her seizing stopped. "She's not breathing!"

"I've got a pulse."

"Bag her."

The pulmonologist fit a tube down her throat, inflating her lungs with air. "Come on Donna," he said. "Don't do this."

Eliza commandeered the STD and HIV investigators to help with contact tracing and interviewing people in the community who might have been exposed to H7N1. Of all the staff at the health department, they knew how to track down people who had been exposed to a communicable disease. They normally spent their days hunting down infected people's one-nighters and internet hook-ups, or trying to track junkies who'd shared a needle with someone who was disease positive in a shooting gallery. They also knew how to break the bad news gently. They were already in the conference room with Geoff and Julia when Eliza walked in.

"So the guy, he asks me, can he catch HIV if he's the second man on a sheep?" one of the HIV investigators said.

"Bullshit. He did not," Geoff replied.

"Yeah. Seriously. I know, right? So I said yeah, I think he could, so he should wear a condom. Or stop fucking sheep."

"That's sick."

"Can you?" Eliza asked.

"Dr E! Always good to see you," the HIV investigator said.

"No, can you? Get HIV if you're the second man on a sheep?"

"Beats me. You're the epidemiologist."

She laughed. "We didn't go over that in grad school."

He grinned at her. "You want me to call CDC? See if anyone's done a study on it?"

"I suspect they've got bigger concerns right now. But I would like to know. Morbid curiosity." While Eliza was very happy that she did not work in the sexual disease department, they did always have great stories.

"So I guess we're working for you now, huh Dr E?" one of the STD counselors said.

"Lucky you," Julia mumbled. Eliza pretended not to hear her, but made a mental note to put her on lab duty. No one ever wanted lab duty. You had to make sure all the samples were collected and packaged correctly, coordinate over-nighting all the specimens to the state lab, and keep up with all the paperwork: what was ordered, what was sent out, what were the results, did all the appropriate people know about the results. It was tedious and boring and a great way to keep Julia out of her hair.

"I'm assuming Julia filled you all in on the situation?" Eliza asked.

"No, but Geoff did," one of them replied. They all knew about Julia's affair with the mayor. Apparently everyone but the mayor's wife knew – but then maybe she did too. A couple of them had applied for Julia's position when it was created. They were not even considered. "What do you need us to do?"

Eliza laid out her plan for finding people who might have been exposed. "We know that Dr Sitala and his wife ate dinner over at Giuseppe's. I need a couple of you to go over there. Find out who worked there that night, see if there is any way we can find out who waited on them. That person would have the highest risk for catching H7N1 from Dr Sitala. And people eating nearby ... maybe they signed a credit card slip? If you can get the credit card slips of the people who ate there that night, we have a software program that we can use to trace back their phone number from their credit card number."

"No way," said one of the investigators. "Is that legal?"

"Yes, it is. You'd be surprised how much legal power we have to work a disease outbreak. Call them and find out if they, or anyone who ate with them that night, have symptoms. Check on all the employees, too. See if any of them have a fever. If they do, I want you to get all of their contact information, name, address, phone number, and then tell them – and the manager – that they can't come to work until that fever goes away. And tell them we know the trick of loading up on Tylenol to take the fever down. I want anyone with symptoms to isolate themselves as much as possible until 24 hours after their fever goes away. I don't care if they don't like it, this is serious. You are going to monitor anyone with fever daily, and let me know if any of them go to Memorial. We can also see about getting anyone with symptoms tested. Anyone from that restaurant develops fever in the next two weeks, I want to know about it. Bribe them with an offer of free drugs," Eliza said.

One of the HIV investigators laughed. "In our line of work, you'd better specify what kinds of drugs we should bribe them with, Miss Eliza."

"Antivirals. I mean antivirals. Give them to anyone with symptoms. Have one of the docs over in the clinic write the prescription. One of the nurses in the clinic can help you figure out the dosages. Got it?"

They wrote down every word she said. "Geoff, I want you to go over to Memorial. I want a list of every health care worker who had contact with the Sitalas. Find out how Michael plans to monitor them. Tell him same thing goes with healthcare workers with symptoms. They have a fever, they get to take some time off. And check on that biology professor, the one Memorial just admitted."

"You want me to go up there? Can I do it by email?" Geoff asked.

"No, I want you to actually go there. The presence would be good. Keep them on their toes. Julia, call Donna Pascoe, Memorial's lab director. I want you to be the liaison between her and the state labs. Keep a database of all specimens that are sent to the state lab and the results of each."

"Will do," Julia said.

"I want a report from all of you in one hour, even if you have nothing to report. Any questions?"

"What if the workers don't want to be isolated? Are we going to forcibly isolate anyone? What about quarantine?" one of the HIV investigators asked.

"For right now, Jack says no. Voluntary only."

"And how well will that work? You know people are going to step out on that."

"We'll see. Hopefully Dr Sitala kept his germs to himself and it won't matter," Eliza said.

"What about the other people who ate at the restaurant? People who paid cash, or someone else bought their meal. How are we supposed to find them?" one of the investigators asked.

"No one pays in cash," Geoff said.

"Sometimes I do," Julia said.

"The public information officer is working on a press release now. I'm afraid the only way to track them down is to announce it on the news," Eliza responded.

"Yikes," Geoff said. "That's going to suck. You know everyone who's eaten there in the last year and all of their friends are going to call."

"Yeah, I know. Jack is working with IT to get a phone bank set up. We're going to get some of the nurses to help deal with the calls."

Back in her office, Eliza found twelve voicemails waiting on her phone. CDC. State health department. Someone from Channel 7 had already gotten wind that there was a problem at Memorial. She felt a tension headache coming on. She forwarded the messages from Channel 7 (they had left more than one) to the public information officer. Let him deal with it. She hated reporters. Out of the hundreds of interviews she had given they never got her quotes right.

She pulled up the city's pandemic influenza plan on her computer and printed it. At eleven pages, she suspected a lot had been left out. She felt a sinking in her stomach and tried to decide what to do next.

Lucy came in with some paperwork for her to sign. "FEMA forms," she said. "They require them on federal disasters. Might as well start using them now, just in case. They are a pain though."

"One of the emails from the state said that the governor is prepared to sign a disaster declaration if we start seeing more cases. I don't think that has ever been done in Texas for a disease outbreak," Eliza said.

Her computer beeped at her. An email from Julia popped up in her inbox, listed as high alert:

> The lab over at Memorial is reporting another case of H7N1. One of their nurses. Also, they think the lab director may have it.

Eliza called Geoff, who was en route to Memorial. "What the hell is going on over there?"

"Not there yet boss. What are you talking about?"

"Memorial has another H7N1. Find out about this. Find Michael. Ask him why we are learning this from the lab and not him. Get her contact information, address, and phone. Find out her status. Was she admitted? If so, make damn sure Michael knows and that she is in isolation. Does she have a family? Kids? Roommate? Secret lover? Find out. If she can talk, ask her. I want to know everyone who has had close contact with her from 24 hours before her fever started until now. Then call her home, well, if anyone from her family is at the hospital you can talk to them there. Either way, talk to her family. Find out who has had contact with her and if they have any symptoms. If they do, I want them isolated. This thing could explode on us. I want everyone in her home on antivirals and anyone else who spent a lot of time around her. Tell them to call their doctor first. If they don't have a doc we can take care of them, but their doc will know about allergies and contraindications and whatnot. You will call them every day for the next two weeks to see if any of them develops a fever. If they complain that they don't have a thermometer, get one from the clinic and take it to their home. But for God's sake, wear a mask and gloves when you do it. Questions?"

"Eliza, you realize I am in my car, right?"

"Yes, I do."

"You also realize I know what to do here, right?"

"I know, I know," Eliza said. "Also, what about the people she was around at the hospital? Her patients? I know that Michael should take care of that. But make sure of it. Any patients she worked with who have been discharged, we may have to follow up on those. Ask Michael how he wants to handle it, if we even need to worry about it. I don't know what department she works in. Oh, and find out what the hell is going on with Donna Pascoe. The lab said she might have too? Geez! You'd think of all people she's be more careful!"

Her cell phone rang. "I've got another call. Let me know what you find out." She hung up on Geoff.

"Dr E. I might have something." It was one of the HIV investigators at Giuseppe's. "A dish washer over here. He was coughing real bad. He called in sick today, told them he thought he had tuberculosis, he was coughing blood. They all want TB tests. They're really confused about why we are here. They said they thought he went to Memorial. We'll check on it when we leave here. Oh, and we don't know who waited on Sitala. No credit card slips. He must have paid cash. That's kind of funny, huh Miss Eliza?"

"Keep me posted." Eliza hoped it was TB.

In the few days since Dr Sitala's death, potential cases of H7N1 began to rack up at the health department. They were waiting for lab confirmation – the lab was taking a long time to process all of the specimens. Geoff gave up coming in to the office in the mornings and just went straight to Memorial. Every morning there was at least one more patient to investigate over there. This morning he'd found a seven-year-old, admitted after he'd left work yesterday. Geoff had the eerie sensation he was holding sand, and his fingers were filling up too fast. What would happen when his hands were too full?

The girl was not in an isolation room, all of them being full. Michael told him yesterday that they were trying to erect some sort of divider, to create a flu ward, but it looked like they had not gotten around to it yet.

From the mother, Geoff gathered that the family had dined at Giuseppe's the same night as the Sitalas. Unlucky bastards.

"Do you know what day she first started having symptoms?" Geoff asked the girl's mother.

"She's had a cough for two or three days. I thought she was getting better, but then it got really bad yesterday afternoon. She couldn't breathe. That's when I brought her to the hospital." The woman stroked the girl's fingers. An IV stuck in the girl's hand, covered with layers of translucent tape. Geoff stood just inside the doorway for the interview with a mask on, hoping he wouldn't catch anything.

"Do you know when the fever started?"

"I am not sure. I didn't take her temperature until yesterday, but she has been acting like she didn't feel well."

"Did she go to school? After she started coughing?"

"Yes."

That's just great, thought Geoff. "Where does she go to school?"

"Parkway Elementary."

Geoff wrote down the information. He called Eliza from the hallway to let her know about the school.

All of the new elementary schools in Dalton looked the same. Geoff hoped the architect was well compensated, although he thought the buildings had a hideous prison-like quality to them. The only way in the building without a security card was through a set of doors at the front of the building, under a concrete archway, meant, he supposed, to be welcoming, but which in fact looked like a giant mouth swallowing the little kids. Inside, a guard of sorts (a middle aged woman wearing one of those cutesy sweaters that make them look fat) sat in what looked like a drive-through window and asked if she could help him. He told her he was from the health department, here to see the school nurse, knowing the gossip would soon fly. She handed him a blue and white visitor's sticker and instructed him to write his name on it and wear it on his shirt. Instead, he had it read, "Hi, my name is Health Department," because he knew that would cause further commotion among the teachers. It didn't matter where he went – no one ever liked to have the health department visit. They all assumed that when the health department came it was to Shut Things Down. Usually for no reason, presence alone indicated they were in trouble. Geoff wished he really did have that kind of power. Although he thought he would only use it for good. Most of the time anyway.

The guard buzzed him through the security doors. He wandered around looking at the artwork that had been taped to the walls. Finally one of the kindergarten teachers pointed him in the direction of the nurse's office. She thinks I am a child molester, he thought, watching her peer sideways at him. He tried to be serious and not crack a joke.

School nurses all look the same, he thought as he entered the nurse's office. Sugary, but not in a sexy way, more in a grandma-baking-cookies sort of way. Especially elementary school nurses. Nurse Janice did not disappoint. He sat down in an undersized plastic chair and explained the situation: one of the students here had come to school with a novel, deadly strain of flu. He watched Nurse Janice morph from happy-go-lucky to afraid. The girl had been in Nurse Janice's office, had sat in *That Very Chair*, had coughed and coughed. Nurse Janice remembered it vividly. She had called the girl's mom, but the mom couldn't pick her up so the child spent the afternoon helping her, drinking a lemonade-flavored juice box and licking envelopes, the results of the kindergarteners' hearing tests that all had been sent home that day. Geoff told her to call her doctor right away.

Fortunately, Nurse Janice kept a log of all of the kids who came into her office, and they could determine who had been around the sick girl. Geoff wrote down the names and had Nurse Janice pull up their contact information on her computer and print it off for him; he would call all of their parents when he got back to the office and advise them of the situation. She also pulled up a list of all the kids in the girl's class and printed that off for him to call as well. When they finished, he asked Nurse Janice to take him to the girl's class to talk to the teacher.

He peeked through the glass window at the second graders, all bent over their desks, hard at work on some project or other. He thought the teacher was pretty hot and wondered if she was single. Nurse Janice went in and told Miss Elmford that she would watch her class for her while she and Geoff talked out in the hall. Geoff explained the situation and watched Miss Elmford grow increasingly pale, and his chances of ever being laid by her vanish.

Back at the office, he showed Eliza the exposure lists and went to work calling all of the parents, while Eliza worked on convincing Jack to close the schools.

CHAPTER 4

Dalton, Texas
Total infected = 2473
Total dead = 28

Jack loved to watch Nabil move, his lithe body like a panther, sleek, smooth. He found Nabil gorgeous. Stunning. So did all of their friends, of course, which made Nabil all the more desirable. "How a troll like you could catch Nabil, we'll never know," his friends teased him. He watched Nabil take a drag on his French cigarette, the cloud of smoke around him made him appear all the more mysterious. Jack took a sip of his drink. Dry vodka martini, dirty. His favorite. Nabil drank a fruity, flavored martini, not really a martini at all, thought Jack, its color that of antifreeze. Music from the jazz band filled the night air. Nabil crossed his legs, tapping his foot to the beat. Jack loved this bar, loved to sit at the wrought iron tables under the trees strewn with flickering Christmas lights year round.

The afternoon's meeting had Jack keyed up, excited. "So then Dr E told me about this crazy policy the doctors over at Memorial developed," Jack said, leaning toward Nabil to be heard over the saxophone.

"Darling, please don't talk shop," Nabil waved him off. "It's so dull. Really."

Jack sat back in his chair, hurt. "Oh. Well. It's just, it's interesting that's all. I wanted to tell you about it."

"Interesting to you. Come on! We're here to have fun. To relax. Forget about work. Be with me."

Jack took a drink of his martini, the vodka cold in his mouth, warm in his throat. He watched the band and tried not to be upset.

"Now darling, don't pout. That's worse than talking about your job." Nabil reached out for Jack's hand. Jack circled his fingers around Nabil's. "I love this band, don't you?" Nabil asked.

Jack nodded and flashed Nabil a sarcastic smile. He winked for good measure. Nabil loved that wink.

"Hello, ladies!" A friend of theirs plopped down at their table.

45

"David! How absolutely lovely to see you!" Nabil dropped Jack's hand and hugged their new arrival, blowing kisses over both of the man's cheeks.

"Hey, Dave," Jack said.

"Dance with me?" The man pulled at Nabil's hands, pulling him up out of the chair. Nabil feigned a protest. "Oh, no, I couldn't. I can't leave Jack, can I Jack?" He returned Jack's wink and followed David to the dance area.

Their bodies twined and untwined, strings tied for a moment in an erotic knot, and untied just as quickly. Jack watched his lover rub his long body against the other man and pretended that it was all innocent.

His phone vibrated on his hip. He checked the number. Eliza. He dialed her, his eyes locked on to Nabil's dancing form.

"Eliza. What do you want?"

"I can't hear you. What's all that noise?" Eliza asked.

"I'm out. What is it?" he yelled over the music.

"It's Memorial. They need help with security. They've got a bunch of people in their emergency room. They all think they've got H7N1. It is getting pretty rowdy over there."

"Why would they think that?" Jack asked.

"Do you not watch the news? Dr Sitala was the top story on the five o'clock. Now the whole town thinks they are dying of an exotic disease. You know how people are."

"Great. Just great. Got to love the news. Fear mongers. Are you at work?"

"Yeah, Geoff's here too. We're going to go over to Memorial in a bit, see if we can help calm everyone down."

"Alright. I'll talk to Grant, and ask if they can get some additional police officers over there to help." Nabil and David returned to the table. They both laughed, leaning closely into each other as they talked.

"Thanks, Jack."

"No problem." He hung up the phone. "I'm sorry," he apologized to Nabil. "Work." He slammed back the remainder of his martini.

"See? What did I tell you?" Nabil flirted with David. "Work, work, work. All work and no play makes Jack a dull boy."

"Just one more call," said Jack. "I promise. Then I am all yours." Although Nabil didn't seem to want him right now, judging by the way he looked at David. He dialed Grant.

"Come with me to the bar then. I am parched, need a drink," David said to Nabil.

"Get me another?" Jack called out after them. If they heard him, they didn't acknowledge it.

Father Kreston sautéed the onions for his famous spaghetti sauce. He stole glances at Cassandra. She slathered butter and garlic onto a large loaf of bread.

"Explain this," she said, brandishing the serrated knife in his direction. "God is all powerful, correct? He can intervene into human lives, that is why we pray. And God is all loving, yes? He loves us so much that he sent his only begotten son to die for our sins. So why does he allow bad things to happen? I'd like to know."

Father Kreston poured a can of tomato sauce into the pan and gave it a stir.

"God could intervene, but there is the matter of free will. He will not interfere with how we make our own choices. We can choose to follow him, or we can choose sin." He ripped up a handful of oregano leaves and threw them into the pan.

"Free will, yes, that's the old argument isn't it, but how do you explain natural disasters? Take the tsunami that destroyed much of the Indian Ocean coast. Flooding villages, at Christmas no less. None of the people living there chose for it to happen."

"Well, no, but there were lots of choices along the way. The choice to build there, to live along the water in the first place. The choice of the government not to have some sort of warning system."

"The choice to drown? Innocent people, who had no say in those so-called choices, drowned."

"Don't pick on my theodicy. We cannot know God's plan."

"That is such a cop-out. And you wonder why I don't come to Mass." She smiled at him. "I guess I will just have to stick to my sorcerer ways?"

He felt his face turn red.

"I have faith in God," she said. "I do believe He is all loving, and He has the power to intervene. I have seen it happen. But I also believe He is a typical man. Full of inconsistencies."

She covered the bread with a piece of foil. "Now move out of the way so I can get this in the oven," she said.

Jack reviewed Eliza's projections for the impact of an influenza pandemic on the city. He skipped over paragraphs on how she conducted her statistical analysis; it was all voodoo to him. The data were outlaid in several tables, how many would get sick (thousands), how many would die (hundreds). The worst part was the projected impact on Memorial. They were screwed. They did not have the capacity to support large numbers of critical care patients, which meant even more people would die.

Memorial had ten ventilators for patients unable to breathe on their own, although one was malfunctioning. Eight of them were currently in use, and the hospital was screaming for more. And kids. There were no resources for kids. They had one pediatric vent – under normal circumstances they stabilized kids that went bad and transported them to the big children's hospital in San Antonio. But Children's was already getting overwhelmed too. This bug seemed to hit kids hard. Not like regular flu. Regular flu typically only took out old people. Sometimes infants. Kids, they got sick, sure, but not this sick. Kids didn't die from flu. Well, rarely anyway. But the Indonesian flu? It was killing them. And fast.

Jack thought he could get some ventilators for Memorial through the state health department. San Antonio had already put in a request for several hundred. Dalton had one hospital for just under 200,000 people, and Jack worried they would only get San Antonio's left overs. Assuming there were any.

He decided he needed a carbonated caffeinated beverage. He dug through the top drawer of his desk for change for the machine.

Before he left his office, he logged on to the state's web-based emergency management software and ordered 100 adult ventilators and 50 pediatric, knowing damn well he didn't have enough hospital employees to support that many. Screw medical school, we may have to train family members to monitor them, he thought. Parents could be taught to change IV bags. *If you want your kid to live....* He shuddered and made a note to have someone start calling school nurses. When the schools closed maybe he could get some of them to volunteer at the hospital. Maybe he could get the state to put them on payroll. I wouldn't volunteer at the hospital, he thought. What a nightmare.

On top of the real patients, they had to deal with the worried well. One of the ER docs had called that morning complaining that they were swamped with worried well. People who had watched the frenzy on the news and decided they too were dying of an exotic flu – even though they had no symptoms. Jack kept telling the news cameras: *Stay home, stay home if you are well, stay home even if you are sick, as long as you can take care of yourself, stay home.* He wanted to add: *Because if you don't have the Indonesian flu, you'll get it at Memorial.* Not that it was Memorial's fault, it was basic epidemiology. Crowd a hundred healthy people in the emergency room parking lot, all cramming to get into the building, and drop one communicable sick person in the middle of them and, well, someone was bound to catch it.

In all the disaster planning, everyone always seemed to forget that in the thick of things people still have heart attacks, still have strokes. Babies still have to be born. And under usual conditions nearly all the beds at Memorial were full, and they had a shortage of nurses and aides. Surge capacity? That was a joke. All the CDC guidelines on disasters called for health departments to increase hospital surge capacity. Well, how were they supposed to do that? Build another hospital? Provide scholarships for nursing students? He thought it was absurd. What should he do when all the beds were full? When patients filled the hallways on gurneys? He had visions of photos from the 1950s, of polio, of school gyms filled with children in iron lungs. When Jack first started working in public health disaster preparedness, an old ER doc gave him this gem of advice:

First world countries can quickly look like third world countries in the middle of a disaster. Don't forget that. He hadn't bought it at the time, just nodded and grinned – we've come a long way, baby – but the idea haunted him now.

He had gotten ahead of himself. He reread Eliza's intelligence report. Memorial had blocked off one wing of the third floor to cohort suspected H7N1 patients. God help you if you didn't have it going in and they stuck you in there. They had 31 patients there now. Six on ventilators. Sixteen children. Four bodies in the morgue, including their lab director. The university was closed, dorm students kicked out. The administration had been terrified of winding up with dorms filled with ill students to care for. Better for them to be sick at home. Some of them had held a protest, a few of their professors joined in – although he suspected that was more about their pay than civil liberty. The school district remained open, despite repeated recommendation from the health department that they close. The civil district attorney planned to meet with the judge and the health authority after lunch. He had drawn up a legal order to force school closures. Judge Brody already verbally agreed to it, he just needed to sign it. Once finalized, the schools would have to close immediately. The superintendent was furious. How dare they? They could keep the schools closed for fourteen days before they had to hold a hearing. Jack wasn't worried about it. He spoke with the school's attorney that morning (off the record, he promised her). She told Jack she thought the schools were crazy for not closing – she pulled her own kids out a few days ago. It didn't make sense. Even during regular flu season most of the transmission in the community took place in the schools. Schools are giant Petri dishes. Then the kids carry their germs home to infect the rest of the family. Children are flu super spreaders. They can shed virus long before they have any symptoms, and can continue for a while after they've recovered.

In her report, Eliza mentioned that the schools were already operating at twenty-five percent absenteeism. Whether that was due to the Indonesian flu or old fashioned fear was an unknown. But a lot of the doctors' offices were reporting cases of flu. Before too much longer the fight with the schools would be irrelevant; they would hit a financial wall. They earned money based on how many students were in class per day. If absenteeism increased they would not be able to afford to keep their doors open.

Eliza also noted in her report that a nursing home director had called her about an outbreak of flu among its residents. They didn't know if it was H7N1 or regular flu. Regular influenza was so hard on the elderly under normal conditions. Should he be alarmed? He wasn't sure.

"Jack, I'm sorry to bother you."

"It's not a problem, Lucy. Come on in."

Lucy placed an armful of paperwork on the corner of his desk. "FEMA forms," she said. "You have a press conference in fifteen minutes. What can I do to help?"

Jack sighed. "You could get me a soda." He held his coins out to her. "Does Eliza know? About the conference?"

Lucy felt bad for Jack. The media were out for blood. They already crowded the conference rooms, spilling out into the hallway with their cameras and microphones at the ready. "She said she would go if you absolutely needed her, but if you don't, she said to tell you that she has plenty of real work to do."

"Typical. If you can get me a health educator who actually knows what is going on, she can skip it. I just need someone who can elbow me in the ribs if I go off course."

"Well, I can do that," Lucy said.

"You want to be on camera?" He winked at her. She probably did know. More than any of the health educators. She was privy to everything that went on in the building. "You keep me from making a fool of myself and you will be my hero."

"Grant from Emergency Management will be there too. You will do just fine." She reached out and took his coins. "How is Nabil holding up through all of this? Bet he's tired of you working such long hours."

"He loves to see me squirm on TV. I've promised to take him on vacation when this is all over. Lord know I'll have enough comp time to be gone a while."

"Hopefully that will be soon." Lucy left to get him a soda to drink before the press conference began. She looked out into the parking lot and realized that it was too late. The reporters were already broadcasting.

Eliza checked her whiteboard. She had four investigators out in the field, tracking down more patients and all the people they had exposed, one at Memorial, and five more in their offices conducting interviews on the phone. In addition to the STD and HIV investigators, she now had most of the environmental health department working for her. She had to make sense of it all, to compile all the data and make reports to the incident command center. Total number of known infected. Number of people in home isolation. Number of people recommended for antiviral medication. Total number hospitalized. Percentage of hospitalized in critical care. Total number dead. The rate of people who caught H7N1 and subsequently died.

It was up around thirty percent. Thirty percent of those who caught the virus died from it. At least among the patients they knew of. She tried to reassure herself – mortality rates always seem high at the beginning of an epidemic because you generally only see the people who are very sick in the first place; you don't recognize mild or subclinical cases at first. There were likely hundreds of people out there infected with the virus who she didn't know about. People incubating and festering. God, maybe thousands. That was epidemiology 101. Still, the high mortality rate bothered her.

Outside her office window, a team of reporters had taken up residence. Was it Channel 8? No. She peeked through the blinds. This was freakin' CNN, updating their live broadcast every hour on the hour. Her head throbbed. She needed a break. She decided to see if Geoff wanted to sneak out with her and go get an overpriced coffee drink. Of course, at this point, she'd much rather have a margarita.

Geoff's head rested on his desk. "I'm whipped," he mumbled.

"Let's take a break. Mental health. Fancy coffee. My treat," Eliza said.

"Are we now past speaking in complete sentences?" he asked, peering up at her. "If so, I'm in. No energy."

They rode in silence. Geoff rubbed his temples. "I'm tired of this," he said, looking out the window at the passing cars, "Let's go find some sheep-screwing orgy. Interview the men involved and determine their motivation. Write a paper on it. What do you say?"

"Works for me. I'm sick of the Indonesian flu too. Drive through or comfy chairs?"

"You're the boss."

"Comfy chairs it is."

They settled into two overstuffed arm chairs in the corner of the coffee shop. Geoff rested his head on the side of his chair in a slouch, sipping his coffee. Eliza used a straw to scoop the whipped cream off of the top of her drink and ate it. "My favorite part," she explained when Geoff eyed her.

"Holy crap!" he said, sitting up suddenly. He learned toward her. "See that woman at the counter? I interviewed her yesterday. She's supposed to be in isolation!" He stood up and walked over to the woman, despite Eliza's attempts to stop him.

"Geoff! You don't have on a mask! Get back here!" Her furious whisper fell flat. She dug through her purse for a mask and put it on. The elastic snapped the soft spot behind her ear.

"Excuse me," Geoff said to the woman. "Didn't I talk to you yesterday?"

A look of recognition spread across the woman's face, followed by panic. Her eyes darted around the room as if looking for an escape route.

"Uh, no, I don't think so." She coughed lightly into her hands.

"Yes, I did talk to you," Geoff said, making a commotion. "I put you in isolation. You have the Indonesian flu and you are not supposed to leave your home!" He stabbed his finger at her for emphasis.

"What's going on here?" the barista asked, her voice a pitch too high.

"She's not supposed to be here." Geoff held out his hands. "She's exposed you all," he said loudly.

"Geoff!" Eliza hissed at him. "What are you doing?"

"It's people like this, Dr E, that keep me at work late every night. People like this who spread disease. Irresponsible! People like this who kill children. And lab directors. And pulmonologists. And school nurses. You should be ashamed of yourself, lady."

"Geoff! Get in the car!" Eliza yelled at him. The woman began to bawl. "Now!

"I didn't mean to! I didn't mean to!" the woman cried.

Geoff stormed out of the shop. The woman chocked into a coughing spasm, which ended with a pool of vomit dripping down her fingers and onto her dress. Eliza spent the next hour calming everyone down and started the latest exposure investigation.

Cassandra placed her ear to the baby's chest. It rattled with each inhalation. "Lots of breathing disease recently," she said. Aside from his rapid breaths, the baby hardly stirred, all its efforts focused on the simple act of breathing.

"How is he nursing?"

"He doesn't seem interested," his mother said.

"We need to keep trying. Father, look in the drawer to the left of the sink," she motioned with her head toward the kitchen. "Get a dishtowel and run cold water over it and bring it to me. Hurry."

She placed one hand on the infant's chest, the other on his head. His fontanel sunk alarmingly into his skull. The baby was dehydrated. She said a brief prayer.

Father Kreston had become a regular visitor to her home during the last few days. They talked every night, they argued. They spoke of God and nature. Cassandra found herself looking forward to his visits. They sat chastely, side by side on the sofa, drinking hot tea, their passion constrained to their words.

But not tonight. Tonight Cassandra prayed over a very sick baby. She took the dishtowel from the priest and held the corner to the baby's mouth. "Come on, *niño*. You need something to drink." The baby didn't suck on it like she'd hoped. She squeezed a drop into his mouth. It dribbled down the side of his face. Out of the corner of her eye she saw his mother wipe tears from her face.

"Oh, God," Cassandra said. She swiped her finger inside the baby's mouth and pulled out a large glob of yellowish mucus. The baby choked and coughed. She took the rag and washed more snot out of his mouth. "No wonder."

She ran to the bathroom and returned with a blue rubber bulb syringe. She inserted the tip into the baby's nose and began sucking out copious amounts of thick sticky mucus, fighting her own gag reflex, squirting it back out on to the dishtowel. It made her want to vomit. The baby's lungs were likely full of it. He was suffocating.

"Mama," Cassandra said softly. "You need to take your son to the hospital."

"No, no, I can't. I can't pay. I can't. Please help him."

I know. He needs to go."

"I can't. I don't have green papers. No white doctors, Cassandra. No."

"Has he never been to a doctor?" Father Kreston asked, alarmed. The baby looked like he was only a few weeks old.

"No, never." The mother twisted handfuls of her skirt in her fingers.

"What about when he was born?"

"No."

Cassandra turned to Father Kreston. Her voice low, but firm. "I delivered him. At home. But now he must go to the hospital. Father, would you drive us?" She gathered the baby in her arms.

"You are coming with us, Miss Cassandra?" the baby's mother asked.

"Yes. We will help you. We will help him." She continued sucking streams of mucus from the hot listless infant.

The sight of so many people in the hospital lawns surprised her. "Father?" Cassandra asked. She reached out to him. "Father, what is happening?"

The priest glanced down at the dying baby in her arms, frightened. "Let's go," he said. He guided the two women through the crowd.

People lined up in front of a long table of nurses, who were clad head-to-toe in protective gear. A woman in a strange yellow spacesuit holding a clipboard walked through the crowd. A man stood near the door with a bullhorn.

"If you do not have symptoms, please go home. We cannot treat all of you." He called over and over.

Still, the crowd did not thin. "Father, please help, we don't have time for this. We need to be inside," Cassandra said. The baby's mother gripped on to her arm tight. She could feel bruises forming under the woman's fingers.

Father Kreston pulled them toward the yellow spacewoman. His attire caught her attention. He watched her eyes drift to the still infant. "He is in respiratory distress, labored breathing, high fever," Cassandra yelled at the space woman. The woman peered down at him.

"How old is the baby?" she said, her words drowning in the motor of her air filter.

"Four weeks," Cassandra said. "Healthy birth. Uncomplicated vaginal. Onset of illness one day ago. Pulse thready."

It startled Father Kreston to hear the Western medical terminologies spilling from Cassandra's mouth.

"Follow me," the spacewoman said.

The trio followed the woman through the crowd to the table. They were instructed to wash their hands with hand sanitizer. It stung the priest's dry fingers. They were given surgical masks. "What about the rest of you? Do you have fever?" a nurse asked. When they indicated they were well, they were escorted into the building.

Four patients lay on gurneys in the emergency room entrance. A boy sat on the floor next his mother, coughing violently. All of the hospital workers and most of the patients were wearing green paper masks over their faces.

"Don't touch anything. If you do, sanitize your hands." The nurse indicated the clear bottles of hand sanitizer on the nurses' station, and mounted on the walls. "If you need to cough, do it in your sleeve. If you feel feverish, let me know immediately." She paused. "Thank you for coming, Father. If I could trouble you." Her composure cracked, her voice became graveled, "if I could trouble you, we could use your prayers."

He smiled a compassionate smile as they walked toward an exam room. "In the name of the Father, the Son, and the Holy Spirit," he said, crossing them both. "God, Heavenly Father, be with us on this frightening night. Give us strength to do your work."

"Amen," the nurse said under her breath. A fat tear rolled down her cheek. "I have never seen this, never anything like it." She motioned for Cassandra to lay the baby on the exam table.

"You are overwhelmed, sister." He could see the panic hiding in her countenance.

"We have a pediatric pulmonologist. He is with a patient. I'll get him for you."

Cassandra took her leave when the doctor arrived. She pulled the priest out into the hallway. "Help her," she said to Father Kreston. "Make sure they give the baby the proper attention. They can't legally turn him away. Not in this condition. If they give you any trouble, ask for the hospital social worker to help you. Insist on it. He should qualify for Medicaid. I can't stay here."

"Cassandra, what is going on with you?"

"My confession. I attended medical school for a while." She sighed. "I knew I had the gift. My mother had it, my grandmother. I wanted to heal people. I turned my back on them, on their ways. Medical school is – was – a horrible place. Call it a clash of cultures." She shrugged. "I was not called to be here." She held her hands up, motioned across the room. "I can't stay here. They do not like my kind. They don't understand this gift."

"God bless you, Cassandra." He kissed her lightly on the cheek and went back into the exam room.

Eliza poured Sophie a bowl of colorful cereal and kissed her on top of her head.

"Good morning. How are my two favorite ladies today?" Steven walked into the kitchen. He poured himself a glass of grapefruit juice. "You ready for a big day at the park?"

"Yes, Daddy." Sophie spooned most of the cereal into her mouth, although a significant proportion spilled down the front of her pajamas. "I need my antenna shoes." She held up one of her naked feet.

"You don't need your tenny shoes yet. You still need to take a bath." Eliza squeezed her daughter, glad to be home after the last week of long work days. She had barely seen her family since the outbreak began.

Steven put his arms around Eliza's waist, holding her close. "It is good to have you at home. We've missed you." He kissed her on the neck.

The last week had been hell at work. More than forty new cases of suspected H7N1 reported. Seven of them died. Trying to contain the outbreak seemed futile as more and more people got sick. Her work days had stretched from eight to ten to twelve or more hours. Many nights she would collapse in bed and realize the only nutrition she'd had all day was coffee and miniature candy bars from the bowl on Lucy's desk.

But not today. Today she would take a break. She needed a break. And Steven and Sophie needed her.

She let herself linger in the shower, the hot water running over her head. *Don't think about work,* she said over and over to herself, her new mantra. *It is ok to take a break,* the crisis counselor told the staff yesterday. *You are no good to anyone if you are in crisis yourself.*

Eliza believed that people who became therapists did so to uncover the root of their own pathos. She didn't have much faith in them. But she did take the day off.

She turned off the water and realized that Sophie had joined her. She sat on the pink and white bathmat pretending to nurse one of her dolls. "Mama, Priscilla needs milk."

"I see that. You are a good little mama." Eliza toweled off next to her.

"Elizabeth!" Steven yelled from downstairs. "Your phone is going off. Do you want me to throw it down the garbage disposal?"

Eliza felt her blood pressure rise, the muscles in her neck and shoulders tense. An ache in her chest. She put on her robe. Fuck them. It was her day off and she would take it. She picked Sophie up off the floor and reluctantly walked downstairs to check the phone.

Michael's number flashed in the display. Asshole, she thought as she dialed him. She hung up before his phone rang. No, she thought. He can call Geoff. Geoff was at the office. Or Julia. Let Julia do some work for once. She turned the phone off and went back upstairs to get dressed.

CHAPTER 5

Dalton, Texas
Total infected = 7114
Total dead = 156

Michael arrived first in the conference room and made a point to sit far from the head of the table. He fiddled with the adjustments on his chair, lowering it somewhat. He brought a stack of papers with him. This is what his job had become – official bean counter for the health department. He kept a database that he emailed daily to Eliza, a list of patients who had been admitted to the hospital with H7N1 (or suspected of it, sometimes it was hard to tell until they had some lab work back, they had seen some patients infected with plain old regular flu too). His list included a host of variables, lab work, treatment, status. The last column reserved for final outcome, discharge or death. Another page in the database log tracked exposures of healthcare workers, which patients the individual healthcare workers had been around and for how long, and whether or not they got sick. If they did, they moved onto the first list.

The others slowly filtered into the room. They all wore face masks, the latest hospital policy. Healthcare workers with direct patient care had to suffer through the day in an N95 respirator, or if they were lucky, a less-stifling positive air pressure respirator. The N95 respirator was a green cup made out of an unwieldy paper that fit tight over the mouth and nose. White elastic bands wrapped over the head and tucked behind the ears. The material was thick, somewhat difficult to pull air through (a total nightmare for anyone who suffered from claustrophobia), but it filtered out H7N1 viral particles, kept the worker from inhaling them and becoming infected. At the end of the day, they would all have a red outline on their faces for several hours. PAPRs were creepy looking, but much more comfortable. A vinyl hood fit over the worker's head. It had a gas-mask like face piece and a hose that ran to a HEPA filter and motor on the wearer's hip. The motor kept the hood inflated with positive air pressure, although the batteries on the things didn't last terribly long. Workers who didn't have to treat patients still wore surgical masks for protection in the building. That's what Michael wore today. A nuisance, but at least he didn't feel like he was suffocating all day. Everyone's eyes and foreheads were the only parts of the faces visible. It made for an eerie scene.

Dr Cromwell took a chair at the head of the table. Dr Kiriarti, the top pulmonologist for the hospital, sat to his right. Michael noted that all of the important people had come this time.

"I know we are all very busy, so I want to thank you for coming," Cromwell said. "I called this meeting for us to strategize how to cope with our growing number of patients. I think it is safe to say that we are operating well beyond capacity. And by the looks of our front lawn," he said, referring to the crowd of people outside, "this isn't going to let up any time soon."

"Probably our most pressing issue is that we have run out of ventilators," Dr Kiriarti said. Michael was disgusted. Of course you would think that, Michael thought. Selfish bastard has no idea what the rest of us are dealing with. Hysterical parents of sick kids. Nurses seeing way too many patients than they can reasonably handle. Everyone well into overtime. No one said it out loud, but Memorial would likely be bankrupt before this ended.

"I lost a patient this morning as a result," Dr Kiriarti said. "I pulled an elderly gentleman off of one and gave it to a young woman. The gentleman died. I stand by my decision, however. He was an old man, with a poor prognosis. The woman is a young mother. She is improving. I believe she will recover. Yet when this is all over, I will – Memorial will – probably be sued for my action. I believe we need to have an official policy on the use of ventilators in a crisis situation."

"Don't we already?" someone asked. "Seems like that would be in our emergency plans."

"We should have, but we don't," Valarie replied. She had taken over the emergency command role for the facility. "I spoke with the health department again, just before this meeting. They have made a formal request for ventilators for us to the State Emergency Operations Center. The state says they are working on it, but they have San Antonio, and Dallas, and Houston to take care of. And everywhere in between. Everyone needs vents and there simply are not enough to go around. The big population centers are getting the bulk of the supplies. We're going to have to make do with what we've got."

"I agree that we do need to have some sort of triage policy. It makes sense to, considering," one of the ER docs said.

Michael thumbed through his paperwork. They didn't want his opinion. He wasn't sure why he had to be here. He noticed the nurse sitting next to him playing a Sudoku puzzle. He could see that she had made a mistake.

"I am proposing the following," Dr Cromwell said. "First, I think all patients over the age of 50 should automatically be denied ventilators."

This created an uproar, as many in the room would be disqualified if they needed one. "Over 50? That's preposterous," Dr Stratford said, himself one of those over the cut off. "If you want age standards, make it over 70. That's where you're the least likely to have a good outcome. Not 50."

"We have to craft a policy that will save the most people. Let's face it, at a certain point we are simply prolonging the inevitable with the elderly," Dr Cromwell said.

"Fifty is hardly elderly," someone interjected. A few people chuckled.

"The problem with that is that we would still have a shortage of vents. How about we compromise and say 60?" Michael said. He could see from Cromwell's expression that he had pissed him off; Cromwell was stuck on 50 as the magic number.

"What are the ethical implications here? Is age truly a good marker of outcome?" Dr Hendikea said. No one responded. "What if we based our model on severity of illness and complications? I recently read a journal article on this very topic, triage in epidemic conditions, I may have it in my office, I can get it if you would like," he trailed off, looking for interest in the faces of his colleagues. Dr Cromwell sat stoic before him.

"Continue," Cromwell said.

Dr Hendickea fidgeted with his glasses. "Yes, well, if I remember correctly, they first considered patients with respiratory failure coupled with organ failure. Those patients should be taken off the ventilators first. Even with significant intervention their outcome is poor. If there is still need for additional ventilators, they should be removed from patients with underlying conditions. Heart failure, pre-existing lung disease. AIDS. Malignant neoplasms. Also patients with severe brain injury, those in a persistent vegetative state. Age-based criteria could then be a last resort."

Dr Cromwell considered this. He nodded and wished that he had thought of it.

"Save the ventilators for the healthy patients. Patients who are the most likely to survive the H7N1." Dr Kiriarti said.

"I am not comfortable with this," a young pulmonologist at the table spoke up, "Denying treatment? What is this, the Memorial eugenics program?"

"We have to deny treatment, one way or another," Cromwell said. "No one likes it. No one is happy about it. But what choice do we have?"

Samantha wheeled the body to the morgue. The woman was covered with a sheet, but her arm had fallen to the side. Samantha picked it up by the hand, admired the woman's French manicure, and tucked it back underneath the shroud.

Memorial housed their morgue in the basement, far from prying eyes. No one wanted to see evidence of death– it lowered confidence in the hospital's ability to save lives. She held her identification badge up to the sensor and the doors opened with a bang. Inside, the pathologist leaned over a dead man. The dead man lay on a stainless steel table. The pathologist wore a variety of protective equipment, rendering him inhuman looking. A monster. Samantha shuddered.

"We have another customer?" he said. "I'm afraid I'm taking reservations; the restaurant is full."

Samantha didn't find him funny. She hated his morbid jokes, hated this duty. "You've better make room. I've got another one in the emergency department."

"Sorry. I am not kidding. There's no more room at the inn. The medical examiner's office said they don't know when they can come and pick them up, so we're all in here patiently waiting."

"Well, what I am supposed to do with her?"

"I don't know. I only work here." He went back to cutting on the dead man. Samantha left the gurney blocking the doorway and started back out of the morgue.

"You can't leave that here!" the pathologist called out to her. She kept walking.

Samantha sat in one of the leather chairs in front of Valarie's desk. "I have a problem," she said.

"You and everyone else in this place," Valarie said. She opened a small refrigerator behind her desk and took out a diet soda. "You want one?" she asked. Samantha shook her head no, but that was a lie. She did want one.

Valarie pulled off her face mask and popped open the can. "I am so sick of spending my days in these stupid things," she said. "Look at my skin. I am broken out like a hormonal teenager." Samantha wanted to do the same, free herself from the awful humidity of the mask, reward herself with a cold soda. But the mask had become her talisman, and she would not take it off until she was safely outside of the building.

"The morgue is full, and I've got two bodies I don't know what to do with," she said.

She watched Valarie take a sip of her drink. Valarie sighed. "So now what?"

"We need someplace cold, to slow the decomposition, or it will reek to high heaven in here."

"Someplace cold. How about the cafeteria, don't they have a big walk-in freezer? We could store them in there, at least temporarily."

"That should work. It won't hold many though," Samantha said.

"Okay. I'll call over to the health department and let them know we have a storage problem. Maybe we can get a refrigerated truck over here. Fill it up and I'll drive it over to the medical examiner's office myself. Those jerks."

Valarie finished her soda and the two women went to the cafeteria. Two large freezers sat at the back of the kitchen. The staff helped them move over as much of the food as they could fit into one of the freezers. Samantha wheeled the two bodies into the other one.

"This will be bad for business, you know," the cafeteria manager told her.

"Isn't all of this?" Samantha asked.

Eliza fiddled with the Lego knight that Jack kept on the corner of his desk.

"I agree, I can see that it's an appropriate course of action, but how would we ever enforce it?" Eliza asked. She took the tiny sword from the knight's hand and waved it in Grant's direction. Enforcement. She had left the 'how to' section out of her original pandemic influenza disaster plan. Instead she'd filled it with what seemed like reasonable enough suggestions. Reasonable when one did not have to worry with the logistics of making it happen. Cancel large gatherings. Conferences, meetings, movies (the theaters were angry at the suggestion), and even worse in Texas, church. Want to infuriate a conservative community like Dalton? Cancel church. Follow it up by cancelling football and then watch over your shoulder for the lynch mob.

"I think we have to rely on the community to cooperate voluntarily," Jack said, ever the peace-maker.

"Do you really believe that people will do that? When Big Blockbuster Movie Part Three is released, and the theaters stand to lose thousands of dollars, not to mention the neighboring restaurants, then what? When people want to go to a crowded bar, to get away from all this? And church Sunday to repent for the debauchery of the night before, which is usually followed by lunch out and a trip to the mall, we tell them no? Sorry, the city is closed? How long will that last?"

"We frame it like a snow day," Grant said. "A voluntary snow day. Schools are already closed, call it Family Together Days."

Jack nodded. "That might work."

"Are you kidding me? Maybe for a day or two. And then they'll get bored," Eliza said.

Jack rubbed his face in his hands and groaned. "Okay. Work with me here. The best way to keep people from getting sick is to keep them apart. How do we do that, if we don't have the manpower to force them to stay home?"

"We'll have to convince them it's the right thing to do. Protect yourself! Protect your family! Stay the hell home! We can't force them. They'll have to buy into it," Grant said.

"You will die unless you stay home," Eliza said.

Grant nodded. "Yes. You. Will. Die. They need to believe that."

"Well, some will. Die, I mean," Jack said.

"They need to believe they all will. There are not enough police officers in the state to force everyone to keep apart. But if we can really instill some fear in them, they'll do it," Grant said.

"So we craft a message: The more isolated you can be, the less likely you'll catch the Indonesian flu."

"No. The more likely you'll live," Eliza said.

"We need to get the public information officer. Blast the message out through the media. Let's get as much media coverage as possible. Scare the crap out of people," Jack said.

Eliza hid it, but this thing did scare the crap out of her. She made a mental note to remind Steven not to leave the house with Sophie, even if she was driving him insane, and tried to stifle her own fears.

While the three agreed on their plan, they had to sell it to the mayor. And the mayor wasn't buying it. "You want me to shut down businesses? That is absurd. I can't do that." The mayor doodled on the yellow legal pad on the desk in front of him.

"Only temporarily," Eliza said. "And only non-essential businesses. Those that provide entertainment, any place that encourages large groups of people to intermingle. Shopping centers, movie theaters, the mall."

Eliza, Jack, and Grant sat in a semi-circle around the front of the mayor's desk. Eliza did not want to come, but Jack thought she could be the voice of authority. He was wrong.

"I believe, young lady, that businesses which provide entertainment would argue with you about their essentiality," the mayor said. He crossed his arms, leaned back in his chair and stared hard at her.

Eliza felt the heat rise to her face, but Grant stopped her from putting the mayor in his place. "Right now, as we speak, the cafeteria freezer at Memorial Hospital is filled with dead bodies because we have no place else to keep them. Their morgue is full. They have requested supplies and extra security to help them cope with the large numbers of H7N1 patients over there. And with all of the worried well – the people who are not sick, but who think they are. And the hospital has run out of antiviral drugs for the patients," Grant said. It was a bit of an exaggeration, but it seemed to have an impact on the mayor.

Not to be defeated, Eliza jumped in. "The people who are sick – they all caught the virus – every last one of them – in public venues. And there will be more, if we don't shut things down."

"The university has already closed for the semester," Jack said. "The public schools will follow suit. Today should be the last day of school for a while." He chose not to mention that the schools had been closed with a court order; the mayor would find that out later. "That should help slow transmission some, especially since children are so good at it. But it won't work if parents take their kids to the mall, or to go see a movie."

"The health department is recommending that the city help with additional closures. We're not going to force it, though," Grant said.

"I understand your position," replied the mayor. "Now try and understand mine. If I were to order businesses to close, that would mean significant loss of revenue. Not just for the businesses themselves, but for us too. We'd lose our income from the missing sales tax. Cities don't run themselves, you know. To top it off, a lot of people would lose their livelihoods. You think those employers are going to keep writing paychecks when their doors are closed?

Don't hold your breath. So then what? People can't pay their rent, their mortgage, their gas bill, on and on, in a domino effect. And who is held accountable? Me."

Grant shifted forward in his chair. "They're already doing it in San Antonio," he said.

"Really?" The mayor appeared genuinely surprised.

"Yeah. That hit the news just a little while ago. Read about it on my iPhone while we were waiting in your lobby. If San Antonio can do it..." Grant didn't finish his sentence.

"And of course, on the other hand, you would probably be held accountable if we wind up with a lot of people sick, and dead, and the public finds out that you chose not to follow the health department's recommendations." Eliza said this with a smug look on her face.

"Well," said the mayor, looking at each of them, one at a time, in the eyes. "You have given me a lot to think about. I will let you know what I decide." He showed them to the door.

"We have a press conference this afternoon at three," Jack said.

"You'll have your decision by then?" asked Eliza.

The mayor looked at her with contempt. "I will let you know what I decide," he repeated.

The townhouse was quiet, dark. Jack flipped on a light. "Nabil? Honey? Are you home?" He walked into the kitchen, opened the refrigerator and grabbed a beer. Glancing into the living room, he saw a figure lying on the sofa.

Nabil was wrapped in a blanket. A wet washcloth covered his eyes and forehead. Jack knelt beside him and rubbed his arm.

"What's wrong?"

"I feel like dog shit." Nabil removed the washcloth and tossed it on the coffee table. He rubbed his red eyes.

"I'm so sorry you feel bad. Do you have a fever?"

"Yes. I don't know."

Jack went to get the thermometer out of the medicine cabinet. He came back and took Nabil's temperature.

"100. A low fever. What's hurting you?"

"I just feel bad. Weak."

"Have you taken anything?"

"No." Nabil never took medicine. Getting him to the doctor was almost impossible. Jack got some aspirin and a glass of water.

"Can I fix you anything to eat?"

"No. Thanks." Nabil swallowed the pills. "How was your day?"

Jack sat on the floor in front of him and pulled off his tie. "Long. I am the world's punching bag, you know." He looked at his watch. "I should be on the news in a few minutes. Want to watch?"

"Of course."

Jack flipped on the TV just in time to see a shot of the front of the health department, the words Killer Flu stamped across it in red.

"You're the top story," Nabil said. "You must be pretty important."

"You know I am." He winked at Nabil and turned up the volume.

"Today we have an update on the killer flu outbreak." A woman in a red suit read the teleprompter.

"More people are dead today as an unusual strain of flu contaminates our community," the man sitting next to her read.

The screen flashed to a close-up of Jack's face. "We are doing everything we can to stop this outbreak."

"Schools were closed today in an unprecedented move," the woman in red said.

Another sound bite from Jack: "By closing the schools we can help limit spread of this disease."

"Meanwhile, employers are complaining about employees who have to leave work to take care of their children," a reporter said. "Are people going to lose their jobs?"

Jack's confidence soared in front of the camera. He stuck with his sound bite. "The most effective way to stop the spread of this virus is for people to limit interaction. We recommend that the public avoid crowds and areas where they might be exposed."

The story transitioned from the local scene to national happenings. CDC had worked with the FAA to cancel all flights to or from the US to Indonesia (no word about how the Indonesians felt about this). Major outbreaks were being reported from Los Angeles, New York, and San Antonio, with sporadic cases in other locales. The governor of Texas ordered closure of all state universities, much to the dismay of football fans everywhere. Dr Melissa, the station's health reporter, came on and demonstrated how people should properly wash their hands. She donned a surgical mask and stated, "While the Centers for Disease Control are not yet recommending that people wear masks, masks will help prevent contracting the disease."

Nabil laughed. "Where does one even purchase a mask like that?"

"We have thousands of them. The average person? I don't know. Off the Internet?"

"I love it. Hordes of people will be storming your doors in search of the elusive mask." Nabil coughed a few times and took a sip of water.

Jack kissed Nabil on the forehead. He changed the channel to a movie and went to make Nabil some soup.

The days always started the same, no matter what day of the week it was. The dog even knew the routine and followed him through the steps. Michael's alarm screeched at 5:45 am. He'd flip it off and stand next to the bed for a few yoga stretches. Then, he'd use the bathroom (for his regular bowel movement), brush his teeth with his sonic toothbrush, rinse with alcohol-based mouthwash, and then shower. He shaved in the shower, a fog-free mirror mounted on the wall, aloe vera shaving cream (he changed the blade every two shaves to avoid bacterial build-up). To finish, he turned the faucets to cold and blasted his body with ice water to close his pores. He then proceeded to slather sunscreen on every part of his pale skin that might encounter the sun that day. Then he would let the dog out back. A miniature poodle. He didn't buy her for her cuteness, but for her hypoallergenic fur (even though he'd never had a dog allergy in the past, he believed it was good to be on the safe side). He was good at that, keeping on the safe side.

   While the dog did her business, he fixed breakfast. One-half cup of granola with almonds and raisins (no added sugar), with one tablespoon of ground flax seeds, mixed together with plain goat's milk yogurt. One teaspoon of local honey (to fight the allergens of local flora). A glass of room temperature water, both to quench his thirst and to wash down his morning supplements. A multivitamin with iron. Additional B complex. Flax seed oil. Glucosamine with chondroitin. Acetyl-L-carnitine and alpha-lipoic acid capsules.

   He laid out his clothing the night before, a habit fostered in childhood by his mother. He kept his watch on the corner of his dresser at night while he slept, the only object that ever adorned it.

   Michael lived in a small garden home with an even smaller backyard. He'd challenge anyone to find as much as a single mote of dust inside. He owned three high-powered HEPA filters that he kept running at all times. Very little furniture decorated the place, and absolutely no clutter. He loved the idea of a minimalist existence and strived to achieve it. He kept bowls of fresh fruit and nuts in the shelves in his kitchen and made sure to help himself to them often. He dedicated one cabinet to supplements and medications, and a pile of first aid supplies. There was a box of condoms toward the back. They expired years ago.

   Michael collected recommendations on how to lead a long, healthy, germ-free life. He ate salmon once a week, for the omega-threes, but not enough to build up pollutants. He ate green leafy vegetables daily, always including a bit of broccoli, even though he hated the stuff. Only whole grains, of course. Free-range, hormone- and antibiotic-free meat. One glass of red wine per day. Four glasses of green tea. And a special filter on the sink faucet to leach contaminants out of his drinking water.

   He exercised daily, on an elliptical machine (easiest on the joints); he had no interest in running outside in the exhaust fumes or in ruining his knees on the pavement. Despite this, he still had a bit of a pot belly. He meditated for fifteen minutes every evening. Most of all, he tried not to let himself get worked up about anything. Stress kills. Of course, married men tended to live longer than single men. They had less overall stress. And the sex. Sex helped for longevity. Still, Michael liked his life. His quiet, fluffy companion. She always happy to see him. She never complaining, never fighting, never working to make him look bad.

After breakfast, he called the dog back inside and fed her. He wanted to get to work early this morning, read his email before checking on the morning Indonesian flu counts. He thought about packing a lunch, but didn't want to take the time to do it. He'd eat something in the cafeteria instead.

He took the car key from the hook near the garage door and then remembered the temporary morgue in the cafeteria freezer, which made him reconsider bringing his lunch.

One of the boys crashed into Dr Stratford. The chart in his hands spilled in a waterfall of paperwork on the floor. "Whoops!" one of the kids said in a sarcastic voice. They both laughed and continued running down the hall.

"What the hell was that?" Dr Stratford said to Cromwell. He bent down to pick up the pages and stuff them haphazardly back into the folder. "Great," he said. "Just great. What are those kids doing running around in here? Where are their parents?"

"Their parents are working." A nurse bent down to help him with the mess. "Those children belong to our employees."

"But what are they doing here? Shouldn't they be in school?" Cromwell asked.

The nurse sighed and handed Stratford his paperwork. "The schools are closed. We have a few daycares, child care centers, set up around the building for the kids." She could tell by the expressions on the doctors' faces that they still didn't get it. "Ok, I know back in your younger days, you both had wives who took care of all the day-to-day family stuff while you toiled at building your careers." She fought to keep the disdain from her voice. "But nowadays, many families can't do that. Nowadays, many women work, and there isn't anyone to stay at home and mind the children. So unless you want half the staff here to leave, to go home with their children, we need to take care of their kids."

She continued down the hall to check on her own brood.

"I told you the nurses are getting bitchier," Dr Stratford said.

Dr Cromwell chuckled.

"What am I supposed to do?" Dressed in a suit and tie, Steven stood before her with the phone still in his hand. Sophie's preschool just called. They would follow the public school's lead and close indefinitely. And Steven would have to miss work and stay home with her.

"Well, I have to go to work," Eliza said, fumbling to insert an earring. "Good God, Steven, I am the city's epidemiologist and all this is happening because of an infectious disease. A virus. I can't hardly call in and say I'm not coming because my kid's school is closed. I was the one who recommended the schools close in the first place." She sat on the bed and fastened the straps on her heels.

"I know, I know. It just seems like your career always comes before mine." He dialed the phone to call his own boss. In reality, missing a day or two probably wouldn't be a problem, but the people at his firm were cut-throat. Few of them had families, and they could afford to work more long hours than he could get away with. Having a family, missing work because of children, was somehow viewed as a weakness, no matter how good his performance.

Eliza listened to Steve as he argued with his boss for the day off. She didn't want to go to work anyway. She would rather stay home and play all day with Sophie. Her day at work would be spent dealing with people just like Steven, people who were angry because no one could watch their kids, people who were fearful that they would be fired for it, people who would take all their anger out on her, while she risked her own life to protect them.

Michael stared at his office wall. Just before the outbreak began, someone in the administration got a bug up their ass and decided that the offices should all be painted a cheery yellow. The color reflected back the fluorescent lights and everyone complained. So they repainted with institution beige. Then the yellow began to seep through, giving the office walls the odd color of bright mud. Nothing out of a decorating magazine, that's for sure, but not altogether unpleasant. On the desk in front of him sat a pile of papers, printed copies of patient charts. Patients with confirmed Indonesian flu, and patients who were suspected of having it. He had to go through them all, enter them into the database for the health department. It was boring, tedious work, and frankly he was sick of the whole mess.

He put a surgical mask on his face and walked down to the third floor. The entrance to the flu ward was blocked off with large sheets of transparent plastic. A make-shift door had been cut into the heavy layers. A nurse sat in a chair in front of the doorway. The table next to her held a variety of protective equipment and bottles of hand sanitizer. She held a clipboard in her lap. She looked bored.

"Hey, Michael, what are you doing down here in plague land?" the nurse asked.

"Just checking on everything," he said. "May I?" He took the clip board from her. On it, she kept track of every person who entered the ward, what they were doing there, how long they stayed, and a check to indicate that they were properly attired in protective equipment. Dr Cromwell was currently inside with a patient.

"Thanks." He handed the clip board back to her. "I'm going in."

"What for?" she asked.

"I've got to check on infection control," he said. He really just wanted to poke around, see if he could catch any of the docs in infection control lapses, call them on some problem or other that needed addressing.

"Lucky you."

The nurse helped him don a gown and two layers of gloves. "You'll need to change masks." She handed him an N95. Michael was claustrophobic. N95 masks made him feel like he was dying a slow death. As soon as it was on his face he could feel himself breathing harder.

"You okay?" she asked.

"I hate these damn things."

"You hate them until they save your ass. There are two layers of plastic. Walk through the first and then close the door. Then open the door to the other side. After you go inside the ward, I will follow you and put a fresh drop sheet on the floor. When you come out, step on the center of the sheet and remove your protective equipment, all but the bottom layer of gloves. Wrap it up in the drop sheet and put it in the trash bin. Come out, put the gloves in this trash bin," she nodded toward the receptacle. "Sanitize your hands with the alcohol-based sanitizer. I've got fresh surgical masks for the building."

"Thanks. You realize I wrote that policy, right?"

"Whatever." She rolled her eyes.

Michael pushed open the doorway to the first layer and let it settle behind him. He felt like he was trapped in a plastic coffin. His breathing quickened. *Calm down, calm yourself,* he thought. He took a deep breath and went through the second layer.

Father Kreston lit a votive candle and prayed. The health department had decreed that there should be no large gatherings, to stop the spread of the Indonesian flu. No large gatherings meant no church services. He didn't want his House of God to be a place of disease, of pestilence. At the same time, how could he turn people away in their time of need? When they looked to God for help? *Lord, give me strength,* he thought. He formed the sign of the cross and tried to decide what to do.

Communion. There could be no communion. He would still open the doors on Sunday, despite what the health department said. He would not close his doors, not now. He already had members of the congregation approach him with wavering faith (and frankly he felt it too, although he tried not to admit it to himself). Especially with all the funerals they'd had this last week. What about the funerals? He couldn't not hold funerals for people. No, he couldn't – wouldn't – close the doors. But he would not hold communion. Certainly no drinking from a shared cup. Surely they would understand? They would forgive him? And the sign of Christ's peace. There could be none of that. As a child, he'd eagerly anticipated that part, silently rehearsing his lines. His heart sped up as he turned to strangers, to shake their hands. "Peace be with you," they would say. "And also with you," he would respond. Although his absolutely favorite part was when the silver bell rang out at the moment of transubstantiation. The bell had been removed from mass for a while, and he missed it sorely, always anticipating the delicate sound when he raised the host aloft. Apparently, so did a lot of others. The bell returned to mass. A delight for him. Now, both rituals must be forgone, at least until the epidemic ended.

His thoughts turned to Cassandra, as they always did when he thought about the epidemic. *Cassandra, lovely Cassandra. Forgive me Lord, but I want to be with her. I want to love her. To be loved by her.* His eyes traveled the outline of the chapel, to the rainbows created by the stained glass, the flicker of the votive candles, the long lines of the pews, and rested on the crucified figure of Christ suspended above the alter. *Forgive me, my Lord. Forgive me.*

Father Kreston met Cassandra three years earlier, just after his transfer to the church in Dalton. He'd come from a small church in Minnesota, in the middle of summer, slammed in the face by the Texas heat. Everyone knows Texas summers are hot, but really, this was ridiculous. He seemed to have a constant trickle of sweat dripping between his shoulder blades, and quickly took to carrying a handkerchief for mopping off his forehead.

The women's auxiliary held a luncheon to introduce him to the congregation. A couple of the women had catered it, he could still recall the tasteless, slimy chicken and the salad smothered with ranch dressing, his introduction to local cuisine. And that cake! Someone had brought a chocolate cake made with Dr Pepper. A strange concoction, but not as awful as it sounded. Cassandra came in late, carrying a basket of tamales. "I thought it was a pot-luck," she said in apology, as people abandoned their chicken for one of her tamales. Father Kreston watched her fix herself a slice of cake, the sunlight revealing the transparency of her long skirt. He thought she had a nice smile.

The women of the auxiliary – the white women – they didn't like her.

"You watch yourself around that one, Father," one of them warned him. The old woman leaned into him and whispered conspiritoriously, "she's a witch."

He laughed at that, realizing too late that he'd hurt the woman's feelings.

"You think I am joking, well, welcome to our neck of the woods, Father. Those Mexicans, they pray to the Dark Lady. They say she's the Virgin Mary, but she's black as coal. Look for yourself, they wear medallions for her around their necks. Graven images of goddesses and whatnot. Heathens. You watch yourself."

He took a sip of the syrupy sweet iced tea and tried to hide his discomfort.

A witch, indeed.

Remembering, he thought it prudent to light another candle.

Dr Cromwell stood next to the crib, watching the monitors as they flashed and beeped the baby's status. He was pleased; the baby seemed to be doing better. The baby's mother sat in a chair next to him. She refused to leave, even though the hospital administration did not want her there. They wanted to keep well people out of the flu ward as much as possible. No point in the mother becoming a patient as well. Cromwell was not used to dealing with parents like this. He usually would have shipped a kid this sick off to Children's in San Antonio. Children's let the parents stay, though, so he would too. He told the administration that if the mother could help care for the baby it would save them from having to find a nurse to do it. He had just started the mother on antiviral medications, but he was skeptical about the effectiveness of the drugs. Several of his patients were not responding to them. And he had quite a few complaining that it made them sick to their stomachs. He had to relieve one nurse from duty because she just could not keep the stuff down and he didn't want her working without it (he couldn't stand the idea of a nurse spreading disease further around the hospital). But this little guy was doing great. He was strong.

The mother muttered to the floor when she spoke to Cromwell, one syllable answers, yes, no. He gave up trying to speak to her when he checked on the baby.

Michael entered the room. "How's he doing?"

"Improving. I suspect we can send him home in a day or two."

"Is she nursing him?" Michael asked, as if the mother were not in the room.

"Yes." Cromwell didn't like the nursing business. He worried for the mother. Such close contact, it was a wonder that she didn't catch it.

"Mrs Garza," he said, acknowledging her presence at last, "Do you mind if we do a lab test on you? Sometimes people catch diseases but don't have any symptoms. Can I test and see if that has happened to you? The test is painless. They just put a big Q-tip in your nose, and check it to see if you have this flu." It wasn't quite that simple, but he wanted her to agree to it.

Michael raised his eyebrows at Dr Cromwell. "Really? You think she might be asymptomatic?"

"She might be. That would help explain how this bug has spread so quickly. Asymptomatic, or sub-clinical infectious carriers. Dr Gordon over at the health department has identified over a thousand people with this. A thousand, can you imagine? That's just the ones they know about. I bet there are at least twice that many infected. Maybe more."

The mother agreed. Dr Cromwell made the request in his hand-held device. "Someone will be here to take it soon," he said. The lab tech assigned to this area came in to collect samples from all the patients who had orders at once, saving himself repeated entrances into the hot zone.

"What are you doing in here, Michael? You of anyone should know it is not a safe place to be."

"Inspecting. Making sure supplies are in place, infection control protocols are being used."

Cromwell thought he was a liar, but he couldn't figure out why he would come in so he let it go. Let the man kill himself.

Cromwell walked out of the room. It had been a long day. Earlier one of his patients had gone into respiratory arrest and died. No one could get to her in time. The baby was the last patient he needed to check on, and it was a relief that he was doing so well. His shift would be ending soon.

He stepped into the alcove and stripped off his protective gear. Once in the hallway he decided to go to the locker room and shower.

Despite closing for classes, parts of the university did remain open. The faculty demanded it, and as long as the students stayed away, the administration allowed it. Many of the professors had ongoing research projects that would simply be destroyed if halted midway. Cassandra pulled at the beveled pewter handles of the library doors, relieved to see them open. Her footfalls echoed across the marble floor. Sunlight through a stained glass rotunda overhead fractured the floor with an orgasm of color. She watched the colors change her skin, a chameleon, as she walked through them. An old woman sat alone at the circulation desk processing a batch of new journals. A couple of graduate students worked over at the database terminals. Other than that, the first floor appeared to be empty of people.

Cassandra approached the circulation desk. "Will you unlock one of the database terminals?" she asked the librarian. "I don't have a password."

"Sure," the woman said. Community members could use the library services, as long as they came into the building; they couldn't access them remotely. When the woman stood up, Cassandra realized she had been sitting on a tall stool; the woman was not quite five feet tall. "Do you know how to use them? I can help you find whatever you need."

"That's ok. Thank you, though," Cassandra said. "Can I print articles from here?"

"Normally no, only students and faculty. But you just go ahead. I don't think anyone will complain," the librarian said. "Business is slow."

"Thank you. Can you tell me where medical reference is housed?"

"Fourth floor, dear." The woman unlocked one of the computers for her. "I'll be just over there. You come and get me if you need anything, okay? I am happy to help."

Cassandra began with a search of the World Health Organization's website. She printed everything she could find on H7N1. Unfortunately, most of it was just outbreak reports, little clinical data, hardly anything about treatment. She searched Medline and Cinal, databases for medical journal articles. She found very little written on the Indonesian flu, the whole peer-review process took so long before the knowledge could be available. She found an early release by a team of pathologists of interest. The authors noted that H7N1 could be transmitted across the placenta and infect the fetus. This did not happen with seasonal influenza – seasonal influenza could not cross the placental barrier – and it concerned her. What would happen to the baby if the mother caught H7N1 in the first trimester, during early formation? She printed that one. Another report, in Emerging Infectious Diseases, noted the cytokine storm phenomenon in healthy adults infected with H7N1. The immune system seemed to over react, and the patients drown on their own immune cells. There were too few articles on treatment. How could she help her own patients? Too much was still unknown. She noted that the attack rate and the mortality rate were both alarmingly high.

The biggest problem with the scientific literature, Cassandra thought, was that it left out the voices of the actual healers. The people outside the formal system, who don't have time to write and publish journal articles. The ones on the front lines, saving lives. The negation of these voices, this was partly why she left medical school.

She walked up the ornate curved staircase to the fourth floor. This area was decorated with Donnated antiques, desks, chairs, art, and display cabinets of early surgical and autopsy tools. Aside from her, the floor appeared abandoned. She wandered through the stacks, the medical texts and paper journals, unsure of what exactly she hoped to find.

In a back corner of the floor, she found a room encased in glass. The Medical Archive room. All of the documents inside pre-dated 1925, many of them went back to the 18th century. An empty desk sat in front of the door. There was a bright yellow notice on the door, forbidding entrance with any materials aside from a pencil and special paper available from the archive clerk. Gloves must be worn when handling the documents; a box holding the purple gloves had been mounted on the wall. Purses, backpacks, and other bags must be left outside in a locker, the keys to which were also available from the archive clerk. Of course the archive clerk was nowhere to be seen. She tried the door. It was locked.

Cassandra dug through the desk and found the key in the top drawer. When she unlocked the door, a light turned on inside the room. She took a stack of the special yellow paper with the strange texture, and one of the pencils, and put on a pair of the gloves to protect the documents from the oil on her hands. She also found a tool for turning the pages, kind of an oversized pair of plastic tweezers with nubs on the tips. She left her things on the desk and entered the room.

A rush of air hit her; the room was under positive pressure. She found old surgical texts. Early obstetrics. Tomes on miasma. She instantly fell in love with the place, all the histories, hypothesis tried and discarded on the road to modern Western medicine.

One section caught her eye: Herbology. Early writings, documentations of traditional healing. All the knowledge that had been lost, she thought. She pulled a few titles off the shelf and carried them gently over to a work table at the center of the room.

The leather covers were so soft, almost corroded. The old books creaked opened and smelled slightly of mildew. She was terrified of harming them. She decided she would like to come back and transcribe these; they were a treasure trove. She found *a materia medica* from the 1700s. Carefully turning through the yellowed crackly pages she looked for anything that spoke of the flu.

On the bottom shelf of the Herbology section, she found a collection of slim medical journals, dated from the mid-1800s through the early 1900s. *The Eclectic Medical Journal.* She opened the earliest copies and read about the Eclectics, physicians who used plants and herbs to heal their patients. *Why have I never heard of this?* She found a selection of the journals which dealt almost entirely with the influenza pandemic of 1918. That made her heart pound in her chest. She leafed through case studies of patient reports, of doctors using an astonishing variety of medicinal flora to treat the illness. She took copious notes. Some of the plants mentioned grew on her property, plants which she had not even considered as flu remedies. A number of tinctures could be used, different portions of the plants soaked in alcohol, the resultant liquid given to the patient in drops. Chest applications had also been used extensively, the medication absorbing directly into the patient's body.

She also found much written on the use of leeches. Bloodletting. She skimmed over that part. While she could find leeches in the stream that ran through the woods behind her back fence if she needed some, she couldn't see patients going along with that. She imagined herself walking through the hospital, slapping leeches on people's chests. Maybe not. She found reference to cutting the chest to drain excess fluid from the lungs. No notation as to the outcome of the patient. She did not have high hopes for that one.

A knocking on the glass startled her. The librarian. Cassandra smiled at her, but the woman did not appear happy to see her here. Nonetheless, she took her time putting the books away. She would not damage them.

She exited the room, bringing all of her supplies and the notes she had taken on the yellow paper out with her. The librarian chuckled. "I suppose I should have let you continue. You treated the books better than most people who do research in here."

"They are fascinating. Forgive me for going in. I'm sure you normally have security on these."

"How did you get inside?"

Cassandra's cheeks flushed.

"Never mind," said the librarian, waving her hands. "I don't think I want to know."

Cassandra picked up her things and followed the librarian back downstairs.

Jack parked his car in the empty lot, in a hurry to get in the building before anyone else. He pulled the key to the pharmacy locker out of the back of his desk drawer and went to the storage area. Inside, he filled his briefcase with drugs: Tamiflu, cipro, levaquin. Samples of mucinex, Robitussin. Codeine. The briefcase closed with a click. When he turned to leave, he realized he had been observed.

"Jack? I thought I heard someone in here," Lucy said. "What are you doing?" She eyed his briefcase.

"I? Oh, I was just getting, I mean, I..." He stopped, the lie wouldn't come. "Lucy, Nabil is sick." His hands started to shake, his body overcome with tremors. He couldn't stop himself.

"Oh, Jack. Jack, it's ok. Sit down." She maneuvered him over to a desk outside the pharmacy locker, and closed the locker door. "Jack, don't you worry about Nabil. He is going to be fine, just fine." She tapped on the briefcase. "Don't worry about this either. I just put some coffee on. You should get some before Dr E and Geoff get to it."

"Are they already in?"

"Yes, they should be. I saw them both pull into the parking lot."

Jack regained his composure and stood to go back to his office. "What would I do without you?" He grinned at her.

She didn't care if Jack liked men. She had a huge crush on him.

He met Eliza at the coffee pot. "Thank God you're here," she said.

He winked at her. "Jack Karl, Incident Commander. Here to save the day."

She rolled her eyes at him. "There's a problem at Memorial."

"Of course there is. What now?"

"They are screaming for more ventilators and the ones you ordered from the state still aren't here. I don't think they will ever be here."

"Christ," he said. "So what do they want me to do?"

"I don't know, you're the Incident Commander Here to Save the Day. I just report what is happening."

"Ok, report."

"They've got seven bodies in their morgue."

"Seven? Doesn't it only hold three?"

"That's right. They've also got a make-shift morgue in one of their cafeteria freezers." She took a sip of her coffee.

"Don't tell Food Safety," Jack said,

"No worries. They want a refrigerated truck for body storage. I called the medical examiner's office and they are overwhelmed by San Antonio. It will be a while before they can come get our dead."

"Lovely. Ok, refer truck is easy. We can probably get one from one of the grocery stores. What else?"

"They need healthcare workers. Doctors. Nurses. Anyone with a vague understanding of medicine," Eliza said.

"I don't know if I can help them with that. I had Julia call all of the school nurses, since they are off work. Out of thirty-seven we got two willing to help out, but one of those refused to help at the hospital. She's coming here to work in the clinic."

"I can't say that I blame them. Why would anyone volunteer to work in a hot zone, where they could potentially bring home a deadly bug to their families?" Eliza tried not to picture her own family. "Without pay no less. I wouldn't do it."

"I think Memorial is going to pay that one nurse. The one that came here is working for free. Three cheers for volunteers. What else you got?"

"You know their lab director is one of the dead?"

"Yeah, I heard about that. That's terrible."

"A couple of the lab techs quit after that, so they are having a huge issue with lab capacity. I called some of the university profs to see if we could get them or some of their microbiology grad students to come help out. I haven't gotten any takers yet." In fact, they practically hung up on her. She honestly thought they would jump at the opportunity. "Memorial also has two sick nurses and a pulmonologist who probably isn't going to make it."

"I thought they had their staff all on Tamiflu?" Most of his staff was on the drug too.

"It doesn't seem to be working. The World Health Organization is reporting a lot of antiviral resistance out of Indonesia and Vietnam."

"Vietnam?"

"Yeah. They are a sinking ship. No health care capacity. Just a lot of people doing their best to survive it out at home. Did you know that no one from the US can travel anywhere in Eastern Asia right now? If you're an American over there, you are pretty much stuck, they're not going to let you come home. There is talk of cancelling all international air travel. CDC is supposed to make an announcement tonight."

"They might as well forget about the travel restrictions. We've already got the flu here in the US. Instead of arguing about air travel they should get down here and help us." Jack glanced down at Eliza's chapped, raw hands, noticing them for the first time. Scabs covered two of her cuticles, and the skin between her fingers looked burned. "Christ, what happened to you?" he asked.

"Oh, obsessive hand washing," she said. "Here's an interesting tidbit. "You know Poteet? With the strawberries? Where they have the big strawberry festival every year?"

Michael nodded. Poteet was a very tiny town famous for strawberries and nothing much else. But the strawberries were fantastic. He took his mother and Nabil to the festival just last year.

"Their police chief decided to cordon off the whole town. He's only allowing supply trucks in and out, and even then he won't let the drivers get out of the truck. The locals open the back, unload it and then send them on their way."

"Not a bad idea, in theory," Jack said. "Don't know how long they'll be able to enforce it." He chuckled. "Don't know that they really have the legal authority to do it."

"Small town Texas. Authority by guns. They are all armed. As long as the community supports it, it will work. As long as Death doesn't come to their masquerade ball they will all be fine."

"What else you've got?"

"Back on Memorial," she said. "They still need more security. They are completely overwhelmed with sick and with worried well. The entire third floor is now the flu floor. They are screening patients in the front lawn. They are turning away most of them, which is really pissing people off, but what are they supposed to do? There aren't enough beds and there is only so much room in the building. I forgot to tell you, one of the guys in the morgue? He died of a heart attack. Out in the lawn. They didn't have anyone to work on him."

"Yikes."

"Yeah, yikes. Do you want to hear about their new ventilator policy? Cromwell designed it."

"I suppose," he said.

"It is only in effect during times that they don't have enough ventilators. Like now. It is very controversial, there was a lot of arguing over there about it. They came up with a formula. The more likely the patient is to die even with the vent, the less likely they are to get one. Anyone with a life-threatening pre-existing condition is denied. After that, anyone over age 60 is automatically denied."

"So if I come in with H7N1 and I already have heart disease?"

"Denied. If you are to the point that you need a ventilator, you are going to die."

"Sans divine intervention."

"Pray away."

Jack could already hear himself trying to defend that policy on the news. *Sorry grandma, but you're gonna die.* "Ok, I'll pass that along to the state. Maybe that will light a fire under them about the ventilators. Anything else?"

"Steven is pissed off at me because he had to stay home with Sophie. Her school is closed. He thinks he will be ok for a day, maybe two, but in the long term, he'll probably lose his job."

"Maybe not. Everyone else is in the same boat."

"He can't see that yet."

"He will." Jack realized his coffee was cold and he had not taken a single sip.

Many of the herbs had begun to die back with the impending winter. Cassandra spotted the bowed heads of the flower she needed among the tangle of flora along the back fence. She clipped bits of the plant, saying a prayer of thanks while doing so, and dropped the clippings into a straw basket. Its medicinal properties were strong; she didn't need much of the plant for the tincture.

The Indian sage grew in great bunches closer to the house. She used it often to treat infections with fever and had learned that the Eclectics had great success with it in the 1918 influenza pandemic. She would make a tincture of this too.

While she harvested the plants, her thoughts wandered to Father Kreston. She'd not seen him since before her trip to the library, but could think of no one else she wanted to share her exciting news with: She had found, rediscovered, good treatments for this flu.

The last time he came over, he got onto her about calling him Father.

"It's too formal. We're friends, aren't we?" he said. "Please. Call me Peter." His eyes softened.

"Of course we're friends, Father," she said. She couldn't bring herself to drop that last bit of formality. It didn't seem right.

Inside the kitchen she pulled out a large bottle of alcohol, the kind she used in her tinctures, from the cabinet. She kept it in an antique apothecary bottle with a glass stopper, for no other reason than she liked the look of it. She drew some of the alcohol from the bottle with a long dropper and squirted it into the basin of her mortar. She washed the sage and pressed it between layers of paper towels to dry. She placed the leaves into the mortar as well. Using the heavy stone pestle, she ground the leaves and alcohol into a paste, thinning it occasionally with more alcohol. She took her time with it, whispering blessings as she mixed the concoction.

The scent of the sage wafted up, filling her kitchen with minty air. She poured the mixture into a glass beaker, filling it about halfway. She added more alcohol, almost to the top, and stirred the mixture with a long glass wand. She would let it sit overnight; in the morning she would strain the plant matter off through cheesecloth and fill smaller dropper bottles with the medicine.

The chest rub would be made from a variety of plants. And boiled onions. Cassandra could remember her grandmother applying packs of boiled onions to her chest as a child to relieve congestion. The Eclectics believed the medicine absorbed directly down into the lung tissue. She wasn't sure that was the case, but she believed it would work no matter the mechanism.

Two different patients had stopped by her house last night, both infected with the flu. Homer had coughed so hard he had dislocated one of his ribs. She felt it protruding off his sternum, heard it pop when she pressed it back into place. She gave him some eucalyptus to help with the soreness. Isabella could hardly sit still. She said that the flu made her restless, like she wanted to flee. "How do you run from your own body?" she asked. Cassandra made her a tea of ginger root, chamomile, and passiflora, which helped the woman relax. Isabella had broken blood vessels in her face, and her eyes were hollowed orbs in a cavern of darkness – the poor woman needed sleep most of all.

Cassandra sat at her kitchen table and rested her head on the cool wood of its surface. She needed sleep too.

Even though she complained about doing it, Eliza enjoyed cooking dinner when she had plenty of time. Pulling together all of the flavors in a symphony of taste. The meditation of chopping the vegetables. The planning, the measuring, the tasting, the checking. An ordered break from the chaos of her job. Today they would have Indian. While the onions sautéed, she made a curry paste using a mortar and pestle out of cardamom, coriander, black pepper, cloves, and cinnamon. She rinsed the rice six times, scrubbing it with her fingers the first three and just rinsing it in cool water for the last three. Their seventh submersion would be in the rice pot. Seven. The number of heaven, she sang to herself.

Steven came into the kitchen and wrapped his arms around her from behind. "Smells good," he said. "I'm glad you're home."

"Where's Sophie?" Eliza asked.

"She's in her room, playing with her babies," he said. "It's their nap time." He sat down at the kitchen table and flipped through a magazine.

Sophie loved playing naptime. In an imitation of nap time at her preschool, she laid receiving blankets out all along her bedroom floor. Most of them were pink, frayed and stained from her baby days. She also had a yellow one and a green one with grasshopper appliqués was a particular favorite. A red, white, and blue one with block letters of the alphabet that they lost for a long time (somehow it had fallen behind the changing table) and still looked new got a place of honor beside the bed and held her favorite stuffed kitty. On each, she laid either a stuffed animal or a baby doll, all face down so she could pat them on their backs with her fat little hands. Eliza loved that part, Sophie being the teacher, whacking the babies comically hard, a crazed replica of the back rubs she got before sleep. *Wham! Wham! Wham! Go to sleep, babies!*

Eliza coated the onions with the curry paste and stirred furiously for two minutes to roast the spices before placing the chicken into the pot. She washed her hands to kill any salmonella bacteria from the chicken, and added in half a can of coconut milk and put the lid on it. People could never figure out where they caught salmonella. They always blamed whatever restaurant they ate at last before the symptoms started, but she believed that most of them caught it in their own kitchens.

"Sam called today. From work," Steven said.

"He did? What did he have to say?"

"They closed the office. Too many people out to keep it open. Other people with kids at home. Or worse, sick family members at home, or sick themselves. He called to reassure me. Everything will be fine. My job is not at risk, long as the company doesn't go under. They are making us use all of our sick and vacation time to pay for the time off. No pay after that. Not sure how people are going to be able to survive. I heard on the radio this morning, a lot of people are being fired if they don't show up for work. Lots of people losing their jobs."

"Well, I'm happy for you," Eliza said, even though she suspected all along this would happen. "Happy for us." She wouldn't say I told you so, even though a part of her really wanted to. Instead, she said, "I'm so glad, Steven. Now you can relax, enjoy your vacation time with Sophie. Where's the spinach? Didn't you pick some up from the store today?"

"I won't relax until you are safe," he said.

"Oh, Steven, please don't make me into the bad guy. It's bad enough as it is," she said. The rice began to boil over.

"I'm sorry. I didn't mean to, it wasn't a dig on you or the work that you do. I just really want for you to be safe. I hate your job. It's too risky. I worry about you catching this virus, this thing," he said. "We love you. God, Eliza, if anything happened. We love you. We want you home with us. Safe."

"Did you remember the spinach at the store today? I am not seeing it anywhere." Eliza asked. She didn't want to talk any more about the risks. It kept her awake at night as it was.

"They didn't have any. You're lucky to have the onions."

"What do you mean?"

"The produce section. There was hardly anything left."

She looked up at him, considering this.

"The whole store was pretty decimated," he said. "Don't you know about this?"

"No, I guess not," she said.

"Yeah, people were talking about it. They said the trucks weren't coming, weren't making deliveries. I can't believe you don't know this, about the food shortages. Go look in the utility room."

Eliza gave the curry a stir and then went to look.

"Steven? What is all this?" The shelves were filled with dry goods. Five-pound bags of dried beans. A twenty-five pound bag of rice. White flour. Whole wheat flour. Corn meal. A row of jars of peanut butter and generic cereal she knew none of them would like.

"Food shortages, Eliza. It took me and Sophie all day to get this stocked up. We went around to all the stores, even drove out to that Piggly Wiggly in Brensville. They're saying there may not be any more shipments. I just wanted to make sure we had something to eat."

The timer for the rice sounded.

Cassandra looked out through her living room window to see a boy running up her driveway. A mangy-looking brown dog ran with him. She walked outside to greet them.

"Miss Cassandra," the boy panted. "I need your help. My nana, please, she is very sick."

Cassandra recognized the boy. He lived with his mother in a dilapidated trailer house up the road. "She has the cough?"

"Yes. My mama does too. Please. I need you to come."

"It's ok, Javier. Let me get a few things. Come inside."

The boy and the dog followed Cassandra into the house. She patted the dog on its head and filled a bag with supplies. The bag was colorful, hand stitched, from El Salvador. It had been a gift from a woman who had come to her with raging diarrhea. Cassandra pulled a selection of herbs from the many bottles and jars on her shelf. She threw some of them into her mortar, and with the pestle, ground them into a paste, and scooped the mixture into a small plastic zipper bag. She grabbed a bottle of her Indian sage tincture as well, and a selection of leaves and stems for brewing.

Cassandra and Javier drove to the boy's home in her truck, the dog happily barking and wagging his tail as he rode in the bed.

A musty, dark smell filled Cassandra's lungs as she entered the trailer. She could barely see in the dim light inside. Constructed in the 1980s, dark wood paneling covered most of the walls. One of the living room walls was decorated with stick-on mirrored panels. Ribbons of gold flake fractured her image.

"Javier, open the windows. The air is bad in here."

As the boy complied, she went into the back bedroom to find her patients.

Both women lay in the bed. Cassandra realized the grandmother was dead. Javier's mother grabbed on to her sleeve. "Priest. For mama. For me."

"Shhh. I am here to help you." She pulled back the blankets, exposing the woman's chest and rubbed the poultice on her. The woman's skin was hot to the touch. The nana had soiled the bed. She wanted to move the mother and clean her, but she was not certain she could do it alone. "This is going to taste awful, but I need you to swallow it." Using the dropper, she dribbled roughly thirty drops of the tincture into the woman's mouth. "I am going to make you some tea," she said, covering the woman back up.

While the water came to a boil she called Father Kreston to come say rites for the dead woman and help move both women off of the deathbed. She was not sure what to do with the body. She dropped a handful of herbs into the boiling water and prayed.

"My nana, you can make her better?" Javier asked.

"Javier." She squatted down so that they faces were level. "Your nana is with the angels now. She is gone to heaven."

The boy's face was blank, but he nodded.

"I need you to watch for Father Kreston for me. Can you do that?"

Still silent, he nodded again and took the dog outside.

She held his mother's head up and slowly poured the warm liquid into her mouth. The woman's eyes stayed closed, but she sipped and swallowed the drink. Cassandra said Hail Marys for the dead woman.

The priest found Javier sitting on the splintered steps leading up to the trailer, staring out at the woods beyond the yard. The boy seemed to be in a trance; he didn't react to the priest's approach. He walked up the steps, watching the boy's frozen countenance, and pushed through the tin door. Inside, he saw Cassandra praying with an emaciated woman.

"Father! Thank you for coming," she said. She walked into the hallway to speak with him alone.

"The old woman, she has been dead for some time," Cassandra said. She wanted to run outside, leave the stench of this place. "Her daughter is still alive. I think she will be ok. We need to move her though. I don't think I can lift her. She wants you to pray for her mother."

"Of course." He looked into the bedroom. "Cassandra, why do you still call me Father? I thought I asked you to call me Peter."

She looked thoughtful for a moment. "There is a line between us. A line, a vow. I care for you too much to cross that, no matter how tempted we both may be," she said.

"I see. Thank you, Cassandra. Thank you for your friendship." He left her standing in the hallway, smiling to himself – she felt tempted too – despite the gruesome task before him.

Nabil stared at the ceiling, his mouth open, greedily gasping for air. His nostrils flared. A talk show blared on the TV: *Which one of these four men is the father of Marissa's baby?* Nabil reached for the coffee table, his fingers grazed the remote. *I'm one hundred and ten percent sure that I am not the father of Marissa's baby! That slut will have sex with anyone!* Nabil's chest sucked inward, his ribs protruding, the muscles in his neck straining, bulging. The audience cheered. Grunting, hyperventilating, straining for oxygen, Nabil

93

grabbed the remote finally, tears spilling from the corners of his eyes, his lips purpley-blue, the TV silenced, the remote falling to the floor. Nabil's back bowed backward, a soft moan escaped his lips from the pain of it, his chest flexed, heavy sucking at the atmosphere, begging the gas molecules to enter his suffocating body. A trickle of blood ran from his nose. The room turned black, with pops of blinding white light, spit frothed out his mouth, that final moment, paralyzed, his mind lucent, his lungs refusing to breathe.

"Honey, you need to get up off that couch," Jack called from the kitchen. He unpacked the latest stash of drugs he'd stolen from work. "Have you been there all day? Do you want something to eat?"

Jack counted out pills and fixed Nabil a glass of ice water. "I got you something that will help," he said.

He walked into the living room and froze. The water glass slipped from his grip, splashing the hardwood floors. "Nabil!"

Nabil's head hung off the side of the couch, his mouth and the floor coated with bloody, mucusy vomit. Jack ran to him, throwing the pills onto the coffee table. They bounced, a few fell on the floor in a hollow exodus. Jack held Nabil's lifeless body to his chest. "Nabil, Nabil." He checked for a pulse, but the body was long cold. "Nabil!" he sobbed.

He reached for the telephone and dialed 911.

"What's your emergency?" the voice asked him.

"Nabil is dead."

"Sir, someone is dead?"

"Yes. My partner."

"Is it the flu?"

"Yes, yes I think so."

"Let me transfer you to body pick up, sir. I am sorry for your loss. One moment please."

Body pick up? Jack remembered, he had just authorized that the Madison High School gym could be converted into a temporary morgue. *Good God, what have I done?*

"Body pick up," a voice said.

"I, uh, my partner, he, he is dead," Jack said.

"This is an influenza death?"

"Yes."

"Ok, sir. The truck is already out, so we probably won't be able to get him until the morning. This is the last run for the night."

"What?" Jack felt like he had fallen head first into some bizarre science fiction story. "You have a truck?"

"Yes, sir. We need the address so we can add it to the morning's route."

"What happens after you pick him up?"

"He will be held in a temporary storage facility until the medical examiner can get to it. The medical examiner will eventually confirm the cause of death, at which point the body can be released to the funeral home of your choice."

"Oh," said Jack.

"What is the address, sir?"

Jack hung up the phone. He would not have Nabil in a body bag in a gym, in a death pile. This was inhuman, and it was his fault. He thought it was a great idea at the command meeting. *Fuck.* He lay on the couch next to Nabil, holding him close. Fluids leaked from the body. Jack cried.

After a few minutes, he went to the garage and took a shovel from one of the hooks on the wall, and grabbed a box of trash bags, the kind he used for lawn clippings. He stood in the backyard. Under the tree, near the wisteria bushes. Nabil loved the smell of the wisteria bushes in the springtime. He used to sit out back on the porch, drinking hot tea in the mornings. Jack plunged the shovel into the earth.

It took hours to dig a hole deep enough.

Inside, he lovingly cleaned Nabil, washing his body gently again and again with a soft wash cloth. He washed Nabil's face, wiping away traces of Nabil's last moments alive. Under his neck, across his bruised chest, the grooves of his hands, the crooks between his fingers, removing all traces of illness. He wiped the excrement that had pooled from Nabil's body as well, the final expulsion of contamination, until Nabil was clean, pristine, beautiful. He dressed Nabil in a shift of green sequins. He painted Nabil's face with emerald eye shadow, cherry lips, and painted his fingernails fiery red. He knocked over the nail polish, its toxic fire staining the wooden floor. He wrapped Nabil in black trash bags held together with duct tape and dragged him to the backyard, and sobbed as he threw shovels of dirt on his lover.

Cromwell glanced over the latest lab reports on Dr Hendickea. There was no improvement in the pulmonologist's illness. He had progressed to multiple organ failure.

"I'm sorry, Ben. I know you don't want to, I don't want to either," Dr Kiriarti said. "But we need to pull his vent."

Dr Kiriarti's eyes were puffy and swollen from crying in the employee lounge earlier. Unstoppable tears, he'd thought at the time, but the faucet had finally shut off.

Dr Cromwell's face hardened to steel, his jaw clenched. He wanted to shatter as well.

Dr Kiriarti placed his hand on Cromwell's upper arm. "He was my friend too," he said.

Cromwell nodded. He couldn't speak.

"You were right about the mother," Michael tossed a lab slip on Dr Cromwell's desk. "She came back positive for H7N1."

Cromwell examined the paper. "That's why this thing keeps spreading. It's one thing if you know who's sick. You can isolate them, put their contacts on preventive medicine, but what about the people who are spreading it and don't know it? Think of every place that woman may have gone, carrying that virus with her. To church. To the grocery store. Maybe she went to see a movie. Everywhere she went, shedding a microscopic killer in her wake."

"Feeling a bit dramatic today, Dr Cromwell?" Michael smiled.

His humor fell flat. "When you become a physician, Michael, and you watch as your patients die, your coworkers die, as they depend on you and your fight to save their lives," he said, "then you can lecture me about my penchant for the dramatic. Until then, I ask for your silence on the matter."

Chastised, Michael left to call Eliza and tell her about the asymptomatic woman.

High school gyms all have the same smell, that teenaged hormone infused dirty sweat smell. Grant surveyed the space. Painted paper banners decorated either end of the large room with school spirit. "Go Mavs!" they read. He thought that was a stupid mascot, the Mavericks. It was a horse, which he didn't really get. Better to be something fierce, a lion or a bear. Or his personal favorite, the Round Rock Dragons. Now that was a cool name for a mascot.

A horse raised on its hind legs, steam marks indicated at its snout, pawed at the scoreboard, painted in blue. Today the gym was silent. He enjoyed how the spongy floor flexed beneath his boots. Bits of blue and white plastic pom pom fodder fray hid under the wooden bleachers, pulled out from the last pep rally. Everyone was really pissed off when they closed the schools. No school, no football. And folks around here lived for football. Despite their dumb mascot, Grant loved to go to the games. Madison had a great coach, and they went to state almost every year. Unlike the university team, which blew.

"Can you show me the climate controls?" he asked the principal. His words echoed in the vast emptiness of the space. "How cold can you get it in here?"

"I'll show you, over here. I'm not sure. We've never had a need for that. Before." The principal opened a machine closet at the far corner of the room.

The colder the room, the longer the bodies would keep. There would still be decomposition, they couldn't bring the temp down enough to freeze them, but they could drop it pretty far. When he was in Kosovo with the UN, Grant encountered tons of bodies that had been left out in the sun. The stench was indescribable. He didn't want a repeat of that.

The State Emergency Ops Center had a guy on his way to help them rig the system to keep the temp really low. This fascinated Grant. How does one get that job, school gym/morgue converter? Did this require specialized training, or was it a self-taught skill?

Probably pays well. How many could there be? Getting the body bags turned out to be easy. The state had thousands of them stockpiled since just after the Amerithrax attacks, for bioterrorism.

"Do you think we will have trouble getting people to come to basketball games after this?" the principal asked, only half joking. Grant felt bad for him. Four high schools in the district and his gym gets picked to be the city's temporary morgue. It had to do with security. Madison was on the edge of town, easier to secure.

"Sure. Coach Jameson knows what he's doing. I'd expect the girls will take us to state again this year. No one will miss that. Of course your floor will have to be replaced. I'm afraid it will be ruined," Grant said.

"It's a nice floor," the principal said. "Cost a fortune."

"I think they'll come to the games," Grant said.

Dr Cromwell stepped into the middle of the commotion in the crowded emergency room. Dr Stratford grabbed him. "They are trying to break down the doors!" Cromwell pushed past him to the ambulance bay. Three EMTs struggled to hold the doors closed as the crowd pushed against the locks.

"What the hell is going on here?" Dr Cromwell demanded. The noise level in the emergency department reached a deafening level. People pushed past him – doctors, nurses, rushing to keep everything under control. Outside, people banged on the glass, their contorted faces screaming for the doors to be opened, to be seen. Patients lay in gurneys all over the hallways. They sat in every chair. A nurse stood next to the nurses' station, frozen, tears streaming down her face. Some of the patients lay on the floor. By the look of the woman on the floor next to Exam Room One, Cromwell was pretty certain some of them were dead.

One of the nurses approached him, yelled in his ear. "They started this a little while ago."

"Where's security?" he yelled back at her. "The police?"

"We've called 911. The police are out there."

The chaos stunned Cromwell. He had never seen such disorder in a hospital. A patient started to scream. The plate glass window next to the bay doors shattered. A crowd of people fell through. Glass shards sprayed everyone in the room, slivers impaling the patients closest to the opening. Those who fell in were sliced and trampled. Bits of glass and blood littered the floor. Cromwell helped a young woman up, her face a jagged slice, flesh pulled from bone. He pushed her into the nurses' station. "Help us!" someone screamed. The horde swallowed him. They rushed about, knocking equipment over, stepping on the patients on the floor.

"My baby! My baby!" A woman in a long hippie skirt held her lifeless infant up to Cromwell's face. He turned from her and tried to flee for the safety of his office. Someone grabbed the back of his lab coat. "Doctor! Doctor! Please!" He fought to free himself from his unseen assailant's grip.

"Benjamin!" He spotted Dr Stratford and made a push through the crowd toward him. Stratford grabbed his arm and pulled him through the people. Someone elbowed Cromwell in the face, a blaze of white hot pain, staining his green face mask purpley red. Blood dripped from his nose into his mouth and pooled inside the mask on his chin. A fist sunk hard into his belly, and for a moment he couldn't breathe. "You fucking bastards!" A young man with round spectacles stood in front of him, screaming in his face. "How dare you lock us out? How dare you withhold treatment from us? And the medicine? Who do you think you are? Fucking gods?" The man held hands with a very ill-looking girl. The girl threw up on the floor. She had eaten Cheetos earlier in the day; the vomit was fluorescent orange.

Dr Stratford pulled Cromwell into his office. The two men fought to close and lock the door. An EMT huddled in the corner. "Help us!" Dr Stratford ordered him. The three men shoved Stratford's desk in front of the door at an angle to prevent it from being opened, and then pushed the leather couch as a barrier to the desk for good measure.

Dr Stratford leaned against the wall and slumped to the floor. "What fresh new hell is this?" he asked.

The EMT peeked through the blinds out the window. "The cops are gassing them." They watched people outside stumbling through clouds of tear gas, copious amounts of snot and tears leaking from their faces. Many lay still on the ground.

Cromwell sat down in the desk chair and slowly removed the soiled face mask. He wiped at the blood with his sleeve. His nose was broken. "I don't know how much longer I can do this," he said to no one in particular.

The doorbell startled Eliza, making Steven laugh. "Jumpy?" he asked. Eliza had put Sophie to bed a while ago. She and Steven sat in the living room watching a movie; it was almost over and she needed to go to bed.

"I'll get it," he said. He could not imagine who would stop by this late, especially without calling first.

It took him a moment before he recognized Jack. He had only been in their home once, for a holiday party. The man was clearly broken, his face shattered, his eyes bloodshot and swollen. Black dirt and grass stains covered his suit, a tear in the pant leg. Dirty bandages wrapped both of his hands, with crusts of dried blood in the weave.

"I had to. I didn't know. Where to go. I need..." Jack seemed disoriented.

"Jack. It's ok. Come on in."

They walked back to the living room, Jack leaving a trial of dirt in his wake. He sat down on the arm chair.

"Good Lord, Jack?" Eliza said. Jack's devastation overtook him. He doubled over and sobbed.

Steven looked at Eliza and shrugged. She mouthed, "Wine?" and he went in the kitchen to open a bottle. Perhaps the wine would numb the awkwardness of the situation, he thought. Perhaps we should call the police? Eliza got up and returned with a box of tissues from the downstairs bath and set them in front of Jack.

"Thank you," he choked, trying to find his composure. He couldn't believe he had chosen to fall apart in here. At Eliza's house. Steven brought the wine and glasses and poured each of them some. He gulped his, hoping Eliza wouldn't notice, and wanted to laugh when he noticed her doing the same, she just as uncomfortable with this late night visit as he.

"Jack," Eliza said, placing her hand on top of his. "What on earth happened?"

He held her hand, squeezed it, and let out a long sigh. "Nabil. Died." The tears started again. Eliza sat on the arm of the chair and rubbed his back.

"Who's Nabil?" Steven mouthed to Eliza.

"His boyfriend," she mouthed back.

Steven threw back the rest of his glass and refilled it.

A few minutes passed before Jack had finally cried all of his tears. "God. I am so sorry for dumping this on you guys."

Eliza hugged him. "Jack, you are a friend. Of course you can come here." She sat back down next to Steven, brushing the dirt from the front of her shirt. Jack reached for his glass and took a sip of the wine.

"He'd been sick for a couple of days. I should have taken him to Memorial, but I didn't think, he didn't seem that sick, you know? Besides, he didn't fit Cromwell's criteria, he had a chronic condition, a heart problem, he wouldn't have qualified for a ventilator if he needed it. If anyone noticed meds missing from the pharm locker, it was me. I've been taking them for him. Didn't help though. He died today at home. Alone. While I was at my stupid fucking job. Incident Commander, here to save the day."

Steven squeezed Eliza's hand. He didn't want her going back to work. He didn't want her involved in this stupid mess anymore.

"Um, Jack? Why are you so, I mean, you're covered in dirt. What did you, bury him in the backyard?" Steven chuckled, hoping his joke would lighten the mood a bit.

"Yeah. I didn't want him bagged in the morgue. An anonymous pile of bodies. Dehumanized." He looked Eliza in the eyes. "We're not saving anyone, are we, Dr E?"

CHAPTER 6

Dalton, Texas
Total infected = 11,316
Total dead = 289

Jack woke up on Eliza's couch just before dawn. His head hurt. He picked up his jacket and walked outside.

The cool air felt good on his face. He fumbled through his jacket pockets looking for his keys.

His own house was cold. Light from the dawn shined through the windows. This was normally his favorite time of day. He walked upstairs to the master bathroom. *I look like a monster*, he thought, catching a glimpse of himself in the mirror. Smears of dirt on his face, his hair disheveled, his eyes bloodshot. He undressed, his clothes falling in a heap on the floor. He turned the shower tap on, holding his hand in the flow until the water heated up and then climbed in, letting the hot water rush over his head until it turned to cold again. He wrapped a towel around himself and lay in a curl on the bathmat.

He tried to ignore the ringing phone. "Jack? Where are you? Are you alright?" Lucy's voice called through the answering machine. "Jack? If you're there, pick up."

He didn't pick up the phone.

A man in a canary yellow jacket walked down the middle of the street, shouting through a bullhorn. "This is the City of Dalton Emergency Management. We are conducting neighborhood checks." As he walked along, pairs of firefighters dressed in white Tyvek suits and gas masks pounded on the house doors.

Sophie ran to the door and opened it before Eliza could stop her. She screamed at the sight of the men.

"Sophie, it's ok baby. It's ok." Sophie hid behind her legs, clutching on to her mother.

"Ma'am, is everyone ok in here?" One of the men asked. She nodded. "Do you have any dead inside?"

"No."

"Anyone sick?"

"No, we are all fine."

"We are asking neighbors to check on each other once a day, and that you call us if you find anyone dead in their home."

"Sure." Over the man's shoulder, she watched the firefighters across the street carry the body of her neighbor out of the house and loaded it into the back of a large truck.

"Jesus," she said. She picked Sophie up and held her tight.

Grant stood under the main tent, watching the rain roll down the side panels and pool on the ground. "Get someone out here to drain that off before it floods in here," he said to one of the men from the church. "Talk to one of the fire department guys. They've got the equipment to do it."

First Baptist Church had supplied the large tent. They normally used it for outdoor weddings. A rental company Donnated the other one. Grant figured neither one would want them back when this was over. He walked outside, not really concerned about the rain, but shook himself off like a dog when he got inside the emergency communications vehicle. A large truck, it looked somewhat like an RV, with huge antennas coming off the top of it. A variety of electronic equipment blinked and buzzed inside; it allowed organizations with different types of radios to talk to each other. That way fire, police, the sheriff, and anyone else who needed to could all talk to each other's radios. They also had computers with Internet access, HAM radios, and satellite up-link in case the whole mess of it went down. Which it had been doing lately. He tried to call Jack again.

Eliza answered. "He didn't come in," she said. "Do you need me to come up there?"

"No," said Grant. "Just do me a favor and tell them at the next press conference that we need some volunteers with medical experience. Any medical experience. I don't care if they are dentists, nursing students, hell, veterinarians would be fine. They can check in by the supply tent."

"10-4," Eliza said.

The police department had finally created some order to Memorial's front lawn. The fire guys got the large tent erected yesterday. It could house fifty patients. Tight, but they could fit. The Red Cross Donnated some of the cots; the rest came from a local camping supply store. Grant tried to get the Red Cross to run the field hospital, but all of their volunteers and personnel had been sent to the Alamo Dome in San Antonio, which had been converted into a mass care center. They had another one set up at a theme park, of all places. But it had huge warehouses and the park's employees had been tasked to help. Grant had managed to convince someone from Fort Sam to give them three more large tents. Those should be arriving soon. First Baptist and some of the smaller churches agreed to help out with meals. Some of them braved working with the patients, but he really needed healthcare workers. In the large tent people could get some supportive care. The worst patients were moved into the hospital.

Grant stood under the awning of the communications vehicle and lit up a cigarette. "Those will kill ya, you know," a passing EMT shouted at him.

"Yeah, well, that's the last of my worries at the moment."

The EMT took cover with him from the rain. "Can I have one?"

The two men smoked in the rain, surveying the lawn.

Cassandra watched the blond woman on the TV. "Literally hundreds of people have come to Memorial. They are camping on the front lawn. Hoping to be seen, hoping and praying, for medical intervention." The woman stuck her microphone in front of a ruggedly good-looking man. "We're asking that anyone with medical experience come help out," the man said.

"You should go, Cassandra." Javier's mother helped her prepare her poultices. The chest rub and tincture seemed to be helping many of the people who had come by her house for help with the cough. "I'll go with you. I'd like to meet that one."

"Neither of us needs to be in the middle of all that," Cassandra replied. "We have plenty of people here we can help."

"I can give them this," she said, closing another jar. "You should go to the hospital. There are more there. They need you. Listen to the man on the TV. Besides, look at him. If he can't be my boyfriend, he should be yours. He is lovely."

Cassandra laughed.

"Or perhaps you would prefer to wait for the company of the good Father?"

"Bite your tongue. He is married to God."

"He may be married to God, but he would like to have an affair with you."

Javier came into the house and the women ended the conversation. As she watched the boy hug his recovering mother, Cassandra decided she would go to the hospital after all.

Cassandra approached a frightening looking police officer dressed all in black, a black machine gun strapped across his back and a black gas mask covering his face.

"I am here to volunteer," she said. He pointed to the supply tent and said something, but she could not understand the muffled response.

The police had formed a perimeter around the tents. At the west end, volunteers in protective gear sat at gray plastic tables interviewing potential patients. A man with a bullhorn advised them to go home if at all possible. Other volunteers escorted patients to the large tent. Some had to be carried. Family members were not allowed inside, only the sick (there is not enough room, she heard a volunteer explain to a sobbing woman). She watched an EMT wheel a child from the large tent to the hospital. A feeding station had been set up at the east end of the complex. Cassandra recognized Lettie's taco truck.

"Cassandra!" Father Kreston hurried over to her.

"Father. I didn't expect to see you here." She felt a flutter in her belly.

"I am so glad you came. They could use your skills." His eyes sparkled over his surgical mask. He led her to the volunteer check-in area.

"You're a healthcare worker?" the man at the check-in table asked her.

"She's a *curandera*," Father Kreston said.

The man looked skeptical. "I don't know if —"

Cassandra cut him off. "I've completed two years of medical school."

"Oh, ok. Great." He showed her where to sign in. A fat woman with a stethoscope thrown over her shoulders and a smiling face drawn in black marker on her face mask came to show Cassandra around.

"You'll need one of these," she said, handing Cassandra a surgical mask. Cassandra tucked the elastic loops around her ears. "You must wear a mask inside the tent and in patient areas outside. Some folk wear them all the time, they're paranoid, but really outside in the fresh air there's really not much to worry about. Just don't let anyone cough directly in your face! Inside, yeah, I worry about that. We've got alcohol-based hand sanitizer everywhere. It will tear up your skin, but you'll want to wash your hands often." She gave Cassandra a miniature bottle of the stuff on the end of a lanyard along with a badge that read 'Volunteer' in blocky red letters. "We've been fighting an outbreak of staph infections inside, another reason to wash those hands. You know how to change an IV bag?"

Cassandra nodded. "It's been a while."

"That's ok. I'll show you. It will come back to you. Like riding a bike. Your job will be to keep an eye on everyone's IV bag. It's glucose water, to keep them hydrated. We can run meds through it too. It's supportive care. Not much more we can do out here. But, you know, we do what we can. Help where we can."

Cassandra surveyed the patients in the large tent. The room was crowded, with little space between the cots to walk. With the exception of an occasional coughing bout, the room was eerily silent.

"I need to keep an eye on all of them?"

The woman nodded. "Yup. Do your best dearie, that's all any of us can do. I'll try to get someone else in here to help with that soon. Let me show you where we store the bags."

She followed the woman out the back of the tent. The IV bags were stored in large lockers. "Compliments of the state health department. They got the manufacturer to Donnate them. Between you and me, I'm really hoping they are not all expired. Let me show you how to change it then."

Inside the tent they looked for a patient in need of a fresh bag. They found one. A man in his mid-30s lay with his arm over his eyes. The fat woman demonstrated how to change the bag, but Cassandra's eyes remained on the man.

"Will you be okay on your own?" the woman asked. Cassandra nodded. "Okey dokey. Well you find me if you need anything, and let me know if you need to leave. When you need a break, let me know that too so I can make sure there's someone to cover IV duty. There's porta-potties and lots of food. Coffee too if you want any."

The woman left her alone with the sick man. Cassandra reached out impulsively to his forehead and held her hand out over it. Her lips moved in silent prayer.

The man grabbed her wrist. "What are you doing?" he demanded.

"I'm a volunteer."

He squinted at her. "Do I know you?"

"No, I don't think so."

He let go and closed his eyes again. "Good. For a minute there I was afraid you were an angel."

She finished her silent blessing and scanned the crowd for empty IV bags.

Eliza and Geoff met Michael in the hospital atrium.

"About time," Michael said. "I was about to give up on you two."

"Sorry," Eliza said. "It's a madhouse out there. Had to park a mile from here."

"And this was probably not the best fashion statement," Geoff said. He and Eliza both wore blue windbreakers, Dalton Public Health written in reflective letters across their backs. "Trust me when I say that everyone out there has an opinion for the health department."

Michael laughed. "That's why I no longer wear scrubs. Or God forbid a lab coat."

They walked through the atrium toward the back of the building.

"How many do you have outside?" Eliza asked.

"At this point, I am really not sure, they come and go. We're set up for fifty in the large tent. The smaller one there, that's for supplies. They've got an incident command post in there too. Area to process volunteers."

"You're staffing with volunteers?" Eliza asked.

"Yeah, pretty much. A couple of the docs go out there, but we try to keep the most critical patients coming inside. Outside is for supportive care. And for people who are toast."

"Toast?" Geoff said.

"Yeah." Michael sighed. "I don't think we are supposed to make it common knowledge, but they are leaving some out there who they know are going to die. Serious preexisting conditions and all. Docs load them up with morphine, try to keep them from suffering, but that's about it. The triage team color codes their charts. First in the building is orange. Orange is for patients who are becoming critical but they are still savable. If there is room, the reds can come inside too. Reds are patients who are in critical shape but might still be savable. Would be savable if we had the resources. Greens and blacks stay outside. Greens are sick, but still doing ok without intervention. Blacks, well, blacks are going to die.

"The triage team goes through the tent every couple of hours, reevaluates everyone's status, patients can go from green to red scary fast. Of course they can stabilize and go the other way too. For a while they were using trauma tags from the fire department. EMS uses them in mass casualty events. It's a card with perforations, you tear off to get to the color you want, attach it with a rubber band to the patient's wrist. The patients wised up though, and they were tearing the cards to orange so they could go inside. Now we use permanent markers on their hands." He chuckled. "Have to guard the markers."

They pushed through the double doors to the hospital's loading dock.

"We don't have a count of how many are hanging out on the lawn," Michael said. "They come and go. I figure there were about five hundred here throughout the day yesterday."

Geoff let out a whistle.

"Probably a lot sent home that really should be here. But what are you going to do?" Michael shrugged.

"We heard one of the churches has opened a shelter for them," Eliza said. "We are going to swing by there this afternoon." They stopped at a supply table, washed their hands with hand sanitizer and put on surgical masks.

Inside the tent, Eliza surveyed the rows of filled beds. A woman near the entrance moaned. "Oh, will you please shut up!" another patient yelled. One of the volunteers intervened. Another volunteer approached Eliza. "Emergency management sent us some crisis workers. They try to keep everyone calm, but you know…" She stuck out her hand. "I'm Jeena." Jeena has used one of the black markers to draw a smile on her mask. Eliza supposed it was meant to be fun, but it was rather menacing. More psychotic clown than friendly nurse.

"Hi." Eliza realized the woman couldn't see her smile through the mask. "We sure do appreciate all the help."

"Want me to show you around?" Jeena asked. Eliza nodded. As they walked by she noticed a slash of black marker across the back of the moaning woman's hand.

"Mostly we try to keep everyone hydrated. If they have meds already, you know, like heart pills or insulin or whatever, we make sure they get that. We try to keep their fevers down. Give them pain reducers. Mostly we're just here for them. They're scared." Jeena's voice caught in her throat.

"You are doing a great job," Eliza said.

110

The woman nodded and wiped at the corner of her eye. "Thanks. Anyway, the triage team will be here any minute. You'll want to see that."

A group of doctors entered the back of the tent. They dispursed like ants across the room. Each patient had a chart attached to the bed on a clipboard, and Eliza realized that despite being housed outside, the physicians were still ordering lab work and tests on them. One of the doctors listened to the chest of a young man lying near her. He flipped through the man's chart, shook his head. "We just had an opening inside," the doc said. "I'd like to move you in. I think we can help you better inside. Ok?" The young man looked frightened. "It's going to be ok," the doctor said. He made a bright orange slash with a marker across the man's hand. As the doctor walked away, the patient smiled at Eliza.

A girl's scream broke through the room. The fresh black mark smeared under her grasps. "No! Please, I'll be ok," she yelled, wiping at the mark. She broke into a paroxysm of coughing, which ended with her vomiting all over herself. Jeena rushed over to clean her up.

A shaken doctor worked on the patient next to where Eliza stood.

"Why'd she go black?" Eliza asked.

"She has metastatic leukemia and kidney failure. Her liver's shot too." He glanced back at the girl. "I have a daughter her age."

Eliza walked back outside. She found Geoff near the supply tent.

"I feel like I need a shower," he said.

"I know what you mean." She felt contaminated too.

An ambulance turned onto the street in front of Memorial, lights flashing and sirens blaring. "Get those people out of the way!" someone shouted. Someone had abandoned a truck about halfway up the drive and people milled about. Staff from the incident command center swarmed out of their tent, rushing to make room for the ambulance. Eliza and Geoff ran to help. Through the commotion, she gathered that the ambulance carried a trauma victim from a motor vehicle accident, a young mother, multiple injuries. The ambulance inched toward the hospital, pushing on through the people. A couple of the doctors opened the back doors and climbed inside. Eliza watched the EMS workers in the back, splashed with blood. It was like watching a movie. A cruel, horrifying, movie.

"This is ridiculous," Geoff said. "Get out of the way, people!"

Finally, the lights and sirens were turned off. The accident victim was dead.

John McMillon bounced around in the cab of the eighteen wheeler. The chair springs poked him through the fabric. He rubbed his hands together. The heater didn't work, and this was the first really cold morning of the fall. He wanted to get back to Atlanta and check on his own family. Shirley kept saying they were all fine, but all things considered, he wanted to be at home.

A guard stopped him at the entrance of Memorial's drive. "I'm with the CDC, Strategic National Stockpile." John held up his ID. "I've got your vents." The guard radioed someone; John could hear the excited voice on the other end of the radio. He moved the barricades and directed the truck to the loading dock.

Grant met them at receiving. "About frickin time," he said, shaking John's hand. "The docs here are going insane for these. What took you so long?" John took this as a rhetorical question. Every place he had been in the last week looked the same, just as messed up as Memorial. He washed his hands with some hand sanitizer.

Light from the neighbor's front porch filtered through the supposedly light-blocking curtains. Eliza tossed and turned, her body in bed but her mind still at work. She couldn't remember the last time she'd had a decent night's rest. To top it off, Steven snored loudly, a grinding, irritating sound.

The bedroom door pushed open and Sophie padded over to the bed. Taking hand-holds of blankets, she hoisted herself up, climbed over Eliza's legs, and nestled between Eliza and Steven. Eliza wrapped her arm around her daughter's small body. Sophie rested her head on Eliza's shoulder and tucked the bottoms of her cold feet against Eliza's belly.

Eliza breathed in the little girl scent of her daughter and closed her eyes.

Sophie's tiny voice broke the silence. "Mama, am I going to get kill? Will that man take me in that truck?"

Eliza kissed her on the forehead. "No honey, you're fine. Don't worry about that."

"Will you get kill?"

Eliza squeezed her. "It's ok, baby. We're fine."

Sophie accepted this and fell asleep. Eliza held her warm daughter and watched the shadows from the trees outside dance on the ceiling.

In the morning, Eliza shut off the alarm and lay back in the cozy nest of Sophie and Steven. "You getting up?" Steven nudged her back awake.

"No."

"Oh." Steven looked at his wife and daughter, wrapped around each other like kittens. "You want me to reset the alarm?"

"No," she said. "I'm not going in."

"Are you ok?"

She propped herself up on her elbow. "I'm not going back."

"Ever?"

"Never. Steven, I can't do it anymore. I don't want to do it anymore. I'm surrounded by death all day. Suffering and death. I keep lists of them, count them, reduce them all to numbers. God! I am so stressed out! I don't want to live this life anymore. I'm sorry. I can't."

"Are you sure? This can't go on forever."

"I thought about it all night. I've got five weeks' vacation time – five weeks! That's insane! Why can't I have a break now and then? But that's a month of pay right there. And really, if we cut back, we've got plenty in savings and when your job starts again we should be able to live off of your pay. Sophie could stay home with me, which would save us a fortune in daycare costs. Besides, if I needed to, I could probably pick up a class over at the university when this is all over. Maybe. I'm afraid they will have quite a few openings after all this. I don't know. I do know that I am not going back to the health department. I mean, I'll go get my pictures off my desk, my diploma. Maybe we can go up there on a Sunday when no one is around. I don't want to see anyone. I don't want to have to explain. What do you think? Is this ok?"

Her eyes pleaded with him, pleaded for him to support her decision. He kissed her on the cheek. "I'm going to jump in the shower. I love you, you know."

Dalton Bible Church boasted having over fifteen hundred members, by far the largest congregation in the entire county. On Sundays, their service could be found broadcast on cable channel 151, their lead pastor known for his inspiring fire-and-brimstone services.

Grant did not go for that sort of thing. He had been raised in a church like that, and could remember lying in bed at night, unable to sleep out of fear that he was damned to spend out eternity burning in a lake of fire. Today he considered himself an atheist. He had seen too much to believe in a God that cared about what happened on earth. Children buried alive in mudslides. Homes with their roofs ripped off, people's life work strewn over miles like so much garbage. Waters rising, drowning everything, people seeking refuge in the same tree as a colony of fire ants. If a God like that did exist, he wouldn't waste his time worshiping it.

He pulled into the church parking lot, which was crowded with cars. A benefit of driving an SUV marked with the words "Emergency Management" and a light bar on top was that he could park wherever he wanted. He pulled up by the front entrance and left his vehicle there. One of the church elders met him at the door. "Thanks so much for coming out," the man said, shaking Grant's hand.

Rogue disaster shelters gave him a headache. They were a double-edged sword. On the one hand, they took the pressure off of the city's response by caring for some of the people in need. The downside though is that they always – always – ended up with more than they bargained for. Then they turned back to the city for assistance and support.

"We knew people would come," the elder said, "but we didn't realize so many needed our help." Grant pulled a surgical mask out of his back pocket and put it on his face before entering the building. He noticed that no one else around had one on.

"Do you have any masks? To protect the people who are well?"

The man shook his head no. "I'll see if I can get you some. In the meantime, at a minimum they should tie a bandana over their faces. You don't want your well folks becoming your patients." He went back to his truck and found a mask for the old man. "You too. Pull it open with your fingers. Put the loops over your ears and then pinch the top down over your nose."

Grant pushed through the double doors into the building. "We have people in the Family Life Center. There's a good sized gym, we set that up with cots, and then we've got a couple of large meeting rooms. We've got people in them too. That's mostly for families with little kids," the man explained.

Grant found the gym. It was much less crowded than the tents at the hospital. Actually, he thought they had a pretty good setup. The cots had several feet of space between them.

"Do you need hand sanitizer?" asked Grant. "I don't see any. I've got a warehouse of the stuff."

"Yes, we would appreciate that. Could you send us some doctors too?" The man's eyes crinkled when he smiled. He knew he would not get any doctors from Memorial, but he thought he would ask.

"I'm afraid I don't have enough myself. Surely you have medical people in your congregation?"

"We have a few working. There's really not much we can do for people here. Make sure they have a hot meal. Keep them hydrated. I think for a lot of them it's just a comfort, you know, having someone to watch out for them. Pray with them. For the ones who live alone especially, but also for those who are just plain overwhelmed. Scared."

"What else do you need from us?" Grant asked.

"Medicines. Antibiotics. Cough suppressant."

"You have a doctor here? I can't give you that stuff without a doctor, you know."

"Yes, sir. I do see Dr Carter over there. Would you like to meet with him?"

"I tell you what. You ask Dr Carter to write up a wish list of what he wants. He needs to sign it and write his medical license number. Fax it to my office." Grant handed him his business card. "Can't make any promises, now, so don't get your hopes up too high, but I'll see what I can do. I'll have a pallet of masks and hand sanitizer for you this afternoon. Do you have a pallet jack?"

"I'm not sure."

"That's ok. They can bring one, I'll just let them know. You'll need to have some folks who can help unload them. The masks, they can be worn until they get damp. Of course you'll want to throw them away at the end of the day and wash your hands real good with the hand sanitizer when you take it off."

"God bless you, son. Thank you."

Grant nodded at him and went back to his truck, eager to get out of there.

Geoff left his car along the street, about four blocks from the hospital. He walked about fifty feet and had to sit on the curb. Each breath caused his chest to ache. His whole body felt weary, drained. He watched a man carry a sick child down the road. The man walked slowly, holding the sleeping girl in his arms. She clutched a tattered pink blanket, the corner of which lightly dragged along the ground. Geoff waited to see if the man would step on it, but it didn't happen. He pushed himself up and followed the man and the girl to the hospital.

Geoff groaned at that the thought of going inside one of the tents. That's going to be an infection control nightmare, he thought. He stopped to catch his breath. A tear ran down his face. *God, I am really sick!* He felt his body lie down on the ground, as if against his will, and curl up into a ball. An insect crawled up a blade of grass near his face.

"Do you need help?" A woman bent down next to him, placing her hand on his forehead. "You are burning up with fever."

Geoff looked into her eyes. His words had all left him. She has a nice smile, he thought, and everything faded.

Geoff reached toward the pain in his arm and jerked back when he felt something foreign. He opened his eyes, disoriented for a moment, and realized he lay inside one of the tents.

"Welcome back," the woman from the lawn said to him. "I was a bit worried that I wouldn't get to talk to you again. I'm Cassandra."

"Hi," Geoff croaked.

"Want me to get you some water?"

He nodded.

She held the cup out to him. He tried to reach for it, but his hand shook violently.

"Don't. It's ok. You're still weak. It will pass. I promise." She held the water to his lips.

"Thanks," he said. "I'm Geoff. With a G." As if that mattered.

"Geoff, it's nice to meet you." She injected a clear fluid into his IV line. "Antibiotics," she explained. "Your flu gave you a touch of pneumonia, but you seem to be responding well to the antibiotics. I suspect you'll be on your way home in a day or two."

Cassandra reached into her pocket for one of her tincture bottles. She had been using the remedy in the tents with some success. She squirted some into a small medicine cup.

"Drink this," she said.

"What is it?"

"Should help with the swelling in your lungs," she said. He swallowed the bitter liquid without further questions, gave her a weak smile, and closed his eyes. He fell asleep.

Father Kreston approached her, finished praying with one of the patients, and touched her lightly on the shoulder.

"It's nice to see one of them improving," she said, looking down at Geoff. "This one has strong energy."

Father Kreston's face looked grave. "I have a favor to ask of you. As a friend. It is ok to say no, if you don't want to. I will understand."

"Father, what's wrong?"

"I've been asked to go to the school. To the morgue. To bless the Catholics. Cassandra, I'm not sure I can do this. I'm, I'm..." he sighed. "I'm afraid."

He looked weary. "Of course I will go with you," she said softly.

"Eliza, we need you!" A pile of requests for information sat on the corner of Lucy's desk. How many were sick? How many dead? How many doses of antivirals did they have left? How many more did they need? When would the schools reopen? At the top of the stack, a one-sentence email from the health department director: *Where the hell is Eliza?* Lucy tangled the phone cord around her fingers. Her phone beeped, the state health department showed on the caller ID for the other line.

"I'm sorry Lucy," Eliza said. "I'm not coming back. I just can't."

"Geoff is sick," Lucy said. Eliza did not respond. "No one can find Jack. No one is in charge!" Her throat caught.

"You don't understand. Every time I close my eyes, I see people dying. I hear a woman screaming because she has been coded black and I can't get her out of my head. I can't sleep. I can't eat..." Her voice trailed off for a moment. "I just have to get out of it all. For my own sanity."

Another line on Lucy's phone lit up. Channel Four News.

"What are we supposed to do without you?" Lucy cried.

Eliza chuckled softly to herself. "Wash your hands." She hung up the phone and pumped alcohol-based hand sanitizer on her own hands, enjoying the reassuring burn on her chapped swollen skin.

Cassandra moved on to her next patient. She changed his IV bag. The old man woke up.

"Cassandra," he said.

"How are you feeling today?"

"Somewhat better. Can you put some more of that stuff on my chest? It really helps."

"Sure." She glanced around to make sure no one was watching her. She carried the chest rub in her pocket in an old Vick's jar.

She dipped her fingers inside and rubbed the herbs under the man's shirt.

"What are you doing?" Michael approached from behind her. She hadn't seen him come in.

"There you go," she said. She pulled the man's blanket over his chest and patted him. "You'll be well soon. Then you can help me care for the others." She turned to Michael.

"Not here," she said. He followed her out of the tent.

"What was that? I saw you put something on that patient."

"It's an herbal remedy," she said matter-of-factly.

"Well, what are you doing with it? Do the docs know you are doing this?"

"I am a healer. A *curandera*. And I believe you will find that my patients have improved."

"*Your* patients?" Michael sighed. "I can't let you treat patients."

"Yes, you can. Healers have been using herbs for thousands of years. Don't you think the world has seen this before? There have been other pandemics of influenza. And people survived. Without Western medicine. Shamans learned from them. It is silly to disregard that knowledge. To let your ego get in the way of saving people's lives."

He leaned closer to her. "Don't let the docs catch you. I can't help you if they do."

Cassandra and Father Kreston walked through the gym, surrounded by row after row of body bags sorted by colored markings. The colors, slashed in permanent marker across the side, referenced the person's religion: red for Protestant, green for Catholic, purple for Jewish, brown for Muslim, blue for Hindu, black for Religion Unknown. Cassandra noticed there was no color for Buddhist; perhaps that had not come up yet. Protestants filled up the bulk of the gym. Two Muslim bodies lay alone near the door, an adult and a small bump inside a large bag, an infant.

They stopped in the center of the room. The priest turned slowly around, surveying the dead. Cassandra held a handkerchief doused with drops of lavender oil over her face to try to block out some of the smell. She tried not to wretch.

"Cassandra? Do you know the difference between terror and horror?" He fingered the black beads of the rosary in his hand.

She assumed that he asked rhetorically, and didn't answer.

"They are not the same thing. When a person feels terror, the response is to run. The movie with the chainsaw character in the room, everyone flees. It is fear of immediate bodily harm. Horror is different. When you see horror, you can't leave. You are glued to the spot, your mouth hanging open in shock, your blood cold, filled with dread. You can't help but look, even though you want to turn away. It's worse for parents. They don't worry as much about their own safety. It's the kids that get them. Tell a parent of a gruesome crime against a child, they'll dwell on it for days. Sometimes they never really get it out of their head. This, Cassandra," he held his arms out wide, the rosary dangling between his fingers, "this is horror."

Father Kreston knelt next to the Muslim baby, and formed the sign of the cross over the bag.

"Father, that child is Muslim."

The priest looked at her with tears in his eyes. "All children deserve God's blessings," he said quietly. He placed his face in his hands and cried.

CHAPTER 7

The state health department welcomed Geoff back to work with some good news. They were getting vaccine.

"It's experimental," Geoff told Grant. "But the FDA has approved it for emergency use. In trials, it seems to be about sixty-five percent effective, so we're not completely off the hook, but it will prevent disease in a lot of people. The bad news is that we have only been allocated 500 doses this round. And I have no way of knowing how much we'll get on the next round, or even when that will be."

"So who gets the 500 doses?" Grant asked, dreading having to deal with the answer.

"It's up to us to decide. Key personnel, of course. You. The docs and nurses over at Memorial. The volunteers working their tent city. People who are instrumental to our response."

"And you?"

Geoff leaned back in his chair, enjoying his new position of authority. He had already moved into Eliza's office and had one of the clerks pack her personal belongings into a box for her to pick up. "I've already had it. Natural immunity is the best there is."

"Security is going to be tough. People are going to flip out knowing that we have a vaccine but they aren't going to get any of it. We'll even have problems among our own people. We can't give it to everyone. And the politics of it, I'm sure that will come in to the mix as well. Administering this may turn out to be worse than not having any," Grant said. "Although I am sick to death of wearing these stupid masks."

"You'll feel naked without it," Geoff said, his face uncovered since his bout with H7N1.

"That's a problem I can live with."

"500 doses. I'll call over to Memorial and see how many they want, critical people only. We'll divide the rest between public health and EMS. Get the police chief, the fire chief."

"The mayor," Grant said.

"Of course," said Geoff. "Can't forget the mayor."

"City council too. You see where this is going."

"I'm going to pretend not to and get a lot of people stuck before that happens."

"You'll be fired. Lose this big new office."

Geoff laughed. "They can't fire me. There will be no one left to do the work."

A shaft of sunlight entered through the window, illuminating a million dust motes that danced in the heat. At the bottom of the shaft lay the grey and white cat that had been hanging around the house recently, sprawled on his back, happy, content, warm. Father Kreston lay on Cassandra's sofa. She had placed an old quilt on him as he slept, handmade by one of her long-lost female relatives, pieced together with colorful bits of dress cloth. He wrapped himself in the blanket and pretended that he lived here.

His dreams were interrupted with the smell of coffee; he didn't realize she was awake. He sat up, reluctant to leave his cocoon of comfort.

"Good morning," she said. "How do you like your coffee?"

"With milk," he said.

She returned with two mugs and handed him one. It had a small chip in the lip. She sat in the armchair next to the sofa and propped her feet up on the coffee table. "I don't think I am going to go to Memorial today," she said. She blew into her cup.

He nodded. "Well, I suppose I should get out of your hair. I apologize for falling asleep on you last night."

"It was a horrible day. You can sleep on my couch any time that you want. I would hope that you knew that by now." She took a sip of her coffee. Her eyes grazed over the sleeping cat on the floor and smiled. "I was not trying to run you off. In fact," she looked directly into his eyes, "I'd enjoy it if you spent the day with me."

Father Kreston felt a surge of excitement. Cassandra. She was dangerous, he knew, dangerous for him. He also knew that it didn't matter. He had fallen in love with her. And while he may not have broken his vow of celibacy in fact, he had shattered it inside his heart.

"I'm giving it up," he said, surprising himself.

"Giving what up?"

"The priesthood."

Cassandra took a sip of her coffee. "You don't mean it. You are just stressed. We all are. You'll feel differently. Yesterday was, as you said, horrifying."

"This is not about yesterday." This was not a crisis of faith. "I'm afraid that I have fallen in love with someone. And I want to be in love with her. I want to be around her, all the time, to be part of her life. And I desperately want to be loved by her."

"You would give it up? The priesthood, for her?"

"Yes. I would."

"Would you resent her for it? Regret it?"

"Never." His eyes pleaded with her.

"Peter." She set her coffee cup on the table and slid next to him on the couch. Her fingers gazed his cheek, and she held his face in her hands. Her eyes filled with tears. "I love you, too."

She kissed him softly on the mouth.

Valarie rubbed the upper part of Cromwell's arm with an alcohol pad. The needle punctured his skin, sunk into the muscle. He could feel the cool liquid disburse into his body.

"Now me," she said, pulling off her gloves.

"I'm not a nurse. I do it and your arm will be sore for a week," he said.

"Whatever, Dr Cromwell. Stick me."

She winced when he gave her the vaccine. "Wow. You're right. You do suck at this."

They had three hundred doses to give out. Enough for their key hospital personnel and many of the healthcare workers and volunteers working outside in the tents. It would cover most of them.

Outside the police fought to keep back the crowd of people who had formed at the check-in tables. Rumors about vaccine had leaked and they were angry. A woman yelled at the nurses. "How dare you! You selfish, selfish people. Folks out here are dying. Dying! And you hide behind your masks, keeping medicine and now vaccine to yourselves! I hope you rot in hell!"

She jumped over the table, shoving the nurse to the ground. Other people in the crowd yelled, cheering her on. They pushed at the tables, toppling one of them over.

A gun shot broke into the crowd. The woman who had pushed the nurse clutched at her arm. Part of it was missing, bits of flesh sprayed onto the people beside her. Blood spewed from a severed artery. One of the nurses ran over to her, jerking off her sweater and wrapping it around the woman's arm. "Well, I guess you are going inside now, aren't you?" the nurse said. She hissed into the woman's ear: "But you still aren't getting any vaccine." She and one of the church volunteers dragged the hysterical woman into the emergency room.

Grant heard the call over the radio after the gun fire. "For Christ's sake!" he yelled into the radio. "Who was that? Get him out of here! No one else shoot anyone!"

He would be glad when the vaccine was all used up, which should be by the end of the day. It occurred to him that he had a horrific headache.

Michael watched the volunteer inject medication into the patient's IV line. "Do you always wear gloves when you do that?" he asked her.

"Yes, always." She smiled at him. He did not smile back. He jotted the information on the legal pad. There are too many patients in this tent, he thought, this is insane. Several of them had developed bloodstream infections, with nosocomial pathogens. Hospital-acquired infections. They also had two cases of pneumonia from methicillin-resistant staph aureus. Those patients had to be isolated from the other isolated patients. So on top of dealing with the Indonesian flu, he had to cope with all these infections.

Seventy-three patients outside. Sixty-one in the hospital, along with more than one hundred patients with a variety of other afflictions: heart attacks, strokes, cancer, and so on. Patients they desperately tried to keep from getting H7N1. And sometimes they succeeded. Others, well, others were not so lucky. But the overall numbers dropped over the last week, by nearly twenty-five percent. Michael plotted an epidemic curve, the number of H7N1 cases at Memorial each day. The curve peaked one week ago. He hoped this meant the epidemic would soon come to an end.

He rubbed the silver talisman hanging around his neck, given to him by one of the volunteers. "Silver has antimicrobial properties, did you know that? Healers used to use silver to stop infections. It seems appropriate that you have it," she had said. An intricate abstract design in sterling; he liked it immensely.

"Hey Michael," one of the doctors called to him. "You need to go inside to employee health. Better get going, before they run out."

Today Michael was supposed to be vaccinated. He had been avoiding it all day.

He stood in line behind a pediatrician with dark circles under her eyes, made more noticeable by the white of her surgical mask. She tapped her foot, impatient for the line to move forward. Michael felt a tickle in his gut. He didn't want the shot. He didn't want an experimental vaccine injected into his body. Just this morning he read a Pro-MED report on complications linked to this vaccine, heart attacks in previously healthy individuals, unexpectedly high numbers of them. Experimental drugs bothered him. Early in his career he did investigations on infants whose intestines had sloughed out from the first generation rotavirus vaccine. FDA had pulled that one off the shelves. Eventually. He could protect himself from H7N1. All it took were good infection control practices. Hand hygiene. Respiratory hygiene. And he, of all people, an expert at avoiding germs, a certified expert, no less, he could escape infection. Another report from the Association for Professionals in Infection Control listserv noted reports of people having seizures following vaccination. Reports had also leaked out of the military; they had some cases of post-vaccination encephalitis. Everyone knew it was impossible to get information like that out of the military, which made him wonder how many soldiers were having problems that had been unreported. Gulf War syndrome all over again. He still believed that was from experimental drugs, anthrax vaccine given to the soldiers. The military. He didn't trust them at all. To top it off, the manufacturer would not be held liable for any adverse reactions to the vaccine. No. He didn't want any part of it.

"I'm allergic to eggs," Michael said.

"You just realized this?" the perturbed pediatrician asked him.

"Yeah," Michael said. He started out of the room. He ran into Valarie at the doorway.

"Did you get your shot?" she asked.

"Oh, I can't. The vaccine is propagated on eggs. I have an egg allergy."

"Since when? I seem to recall your having seasonal flu shots."

He didn't respond, and kept walking out of the room.

Lucy stopped Jack in the entryway. "Jack! Thank God you're back! Where have you been?"

He'd been sitting around his house staring into the backyard. He'd spent most of the time since Nabil's death sitting, staring out the window at the backyard. Until this morning, when he'd inexplicably gotten up, gotten dressed, and found himself here.

"I need to talk to Eliza."

"She quit, Jack."

"What?" The lines around Lucy's eyes looked deeper than he'd remembered. Her appearance seemed faded.

"A lot has happened since you left. Geoff is the Chief Epidemiologist now. He's in his office. Her old office."

"I see." He started down the hall.

"Jack? How is Nabil?"

"He's dead," he called back to her.

The state health department allocated ten thousand additional doses of vaccine to the City of Dalton. Before any of the emergency management staff knew it was happening, the Governor of Texas announced it during a press conference. He read the name of each city, along with the total number of doses each would receive. And Jack was furious about it. Because now he had a city of two hundred thousand people clamoring for his vaccine supply, with no time to prepare for how they would distribute it. Already hoards of people had queued in front of the health department like they were after concert tickets, despite his having staff members walk through them all, yelling through bullhorns that they had not yet received the vaccine, they had no estimated time – or date – of arrival from the state, and that the vaccine would not be given to the public at the health department anyway. Vaccines would be administered at alternate centers around the city. All would be announced on TV, so please, everyone, go home. But no. They stayed. Some brought lawn chairs.

Working with emergency management and the police department, Jack and his team had preidentified locations for dispensing medications after the anthrax attacks in 2001. They wrote a plan, nearly two hundred pages, *The City of Dalton Mass Drug Dispensing Standard Operating Procedure*, bound it in a notebook and put it on a shelf in the conference room.

Jack thumbed through the pages, the tops of which were coated in a layer of dust. He had forgotten many of the details of the plan. Through a convoluted formula he could no longer remember, they had decided in the plan to open ten points of dispensing strategically located around the city to get drugs into people should there be a bioterrorism attack. At that time none of them thought it likely, but a plan was required to receive federal funds to boost their police and fire departments. The pods, as they called them, would run for twenty-four hours straight, with three shifts of thirty staff members each. Well, not staff members exactly. The pods would be run with volunteers.

Problem was that he had no pool of volunteers to draw from. Any there had been were helping out over at Memorial.

He scrapped the twenty-four hour idea and decided the pods would run for eight hours total. One shift. He didn't even have the staff for that. He looked over the pod sites. Madison High was out. So was the bible church. The rest of them included schools and the civic center. But crowding sick people in an enclosed area? Didn't sound like a good idea to him. He decided they would have five pods, all held outdoors. In football fields, well, not at Madison, and maybe the soccer fields through the parks and rec department. The football stadium over at the university. None of this was included in the official plan. He pulled out a legal pad and scratched out his new plan, the revised plan.

Vaccine would go to Memorial first, and to city services, to catch people who had not been vaccinated on the first round. Also, he'd give it to all of their families. Family members of people who were putting their lives on the line fighting this thing, they should get priority too. He would hold a thousand doses back for families. The rest would go to the pods. What was left.

At the pods, they would screen for risk factors. The higher risk somebody had for complications of the flu, the higher priority they had to vaccinate them. People with chronic diseases. All children under age five. Pregnant women. First come, first serve. An ethical nightmare. A security nightmare.

Still, he didn't know who would actually administer all these shots. He picked up the phone and dialed Grant.

"You just need them to give shots, right?" Grant asked.

"Yes."

"Ok, so who besides doctors and nurses can give shots? What about dentists?"

"Yeah, that might work," Jack said, working it out in his mind. "Pharmacists, they can give shots."

"Veterinarians."

Jack balked at that, although he supposed they would be better than nothing. "Can you get the word out? Tell them vaccinators will get priority treatment. So will their families. Be first in line. That would be good incentive for me. Would have been."

Grant missed the last comment. "How many you think you'll need?"

"I'm not sure exactly. The more the merrier, but we'll take what we can get. We'll assign someone here to keep track of them."

"No, don't. I've got something you'll love. I'll have them come here. We can make them ID badges with their picture and everything, scan the badge and give them their work assignment. Scan them out when they leave. We have a program specifically for this sort of thing. We use it with other fire and police departments when we call them in for mutual aid. The system will also run a background check on them, right there on the spot, make sure they aren't child molesters or anything. Make sure they are licensed."

"I'm impressed."

"Your homeland security dollars at work, my friend."

Michael waited in the hall for Cromwell to finish with the patient. He traced the outline of the amulet Cassandra had given him, its silver cool and reassuring on his fingers.

Cromwell exited the patient's room and proceeded to remove his protective equipment.

"Do you have a minute?" Michael asked.

Cromwell nodded. He wadded up his paper gown and tossed it in the receptacle by the door, followed by his mask and gloves.

"I'd like to speak with you about one of our volunteers. She's working outside, in the tents? She's a *curandera*."

"A what?" Cromwell squirted hand sanitizer onto his hands.

"A natural healer. Hispanic healer. You know, they use herbs and aromatherapy and stuff?"

Cromwell snorted at this.

"At any rate," Michael said, "She has this concoction she uses on the patient's chests, she made it, and, well, they seem to be getting better because of it."

Cromwell sighed. "You have a volunteer who is out there giving unauthorized medications to our patients? This is what you came to tell me? Get security. Just remove her."

"No. That's not what I meant. I think she is healing them. Whatever she is using, it seems to be working."

"Michael, I have been in this business a long time. I have heard about all sorts of quackery. Don't you think if rubbing, what did you say, *herbs* on someone's chest worked it would be well known? That it would be documented somewhere in the scientific literature? That the drug companies would be using it, selling it, marketing it?"

"Well, I suppose, I mean, that would make sense."

"This hospital is run on science, on evidence-based medicine, not tomfoolery and voodoo. Send her on her way. The last thing we need is some free-lancer poisoning our patients."

Michael nodded in agreement, but decided he would not tell her to go.

"Do you have Jack's pod plan?" Geoff asked.

Julia looked up from her computer. "I saw his email. I haven't had a chance to read it."

"I need you to figure out what supplies they need at each of the sites – there are references in the appendix, at the back of the plan. Figure out what we've got and what we're missing. Anything we're missing, call the emergency operations center and tell them, they'll get it for us. Jack has a clinic manual for each site, they're out in the shed, bring those in as well."

She sighed. "No problem."

"You know, instead of calling, why don't you just go out there?"

"To the EOC?" she said.

He nodded and left her office.

She wrote a quick text message, *I hate my job*, and sent it to the man who had given it to her.

Dinner tonight? he responded.

She smirked at that.

Julia completed Geoff's errands and then drove over to the EOC. Before going inside, she checked her appearance in the rear-view mirror and applied some more of her favorite glossy lipstick. She tucked her hair behind her ears. *Does this look more professional?* Then she decided she didn't care. Dinner tonight with her lover. At least she had something to look forward to.

She entered the drab government building and immediately felt depressed. She hated working for the city. God forbid anyone use a decent shade of paint. They must get this drab at a discount. The alcove was pathetic, a gross shade of blah. Two thread-worn chairs stood side by side at attention, one of them with a grease stain on the seat. At least she hoped it was grease. They were flanked at either end with metal tables. A lamp perched on one of them, its cord dangling down to the floor in search of an outlet. The other table was stacked high with magazines about guns. *Cheery.* She had to ring the bell at the window twice before someone would buzz her back into the emergency operations center.

A squirrely little EMT lead her through the chaos. She towered over him in her stilettos, which allowed her a nice view of his comb-over. She had no interest whatsoever in men like that, small, and weak. Now Grant, she could easily warm up to him. He stood at the front of the room barking orders to the others, who unquestionably obeyed. She found it very sexy. She swirled her hair from behind her ears. Fuck professional.

"Julia!" Grant motioned for her to join him. She stepped gingerly through the hullabaloo – people on phones, shouting across the room at each other, writing on whiteboards and then swiping it off. A beehive. An anthill. *The queen is here*, she thought, and smiled to herself.

Grant placed his hand on the small of her back, an overly friendly, but not unwelcome, greeting. She arched her back in response, not too much, she thought, just enough to pique his interest. "Glad you could make it," Grant said. "I have a work area for you, here, near me." He led her over to one of the work stations, a small table with a phone and laptop with the Internet running.

"Jack said I should take a look at an EOC manual. Do you have the manual, Grant?" She flirted mercilessly.

"It's on the table." He turned away from her to talk to someone else. She realized he'd already forgotten her. She sat at the table and pouted.

Eliza did check in on her neighbors as promised. Except for the house across the street.

"Don't you work at the health department?" the woman next door asked her. She didn't know any of her neighbors well. Their interactions had been limited to the occasional wave between the car and the house, or running into each other at the mailbox with a bit of chit-chatty small talk. It surprised her that the woman knew anything about her; she certainly could not claim the same.

"Yes. I mean, I used to. I quit."

"I've seen you on the news," the woman said.

"They said we should check on each other," said Eliza.

"My little girl, I think she's had it. She was sick, but not bad. Not like on the TV."

"Oh," said Eliza, not knowing how to handle this, this neighborly layperson role. She didn't want to be the expert, the advice giver, the go-to person in the neighborhood. "Did you take her to the doctor?"

"No. She coughed a lot, but it only lasted a day or two. She did have a bit of a fever, that's gone away, but she has not been acting sick, you know? It never stopped her from playing. So I haven't been all that worried. But after that," she indicated to the house across the street. "That gave me the willies! Has kept me up staring at her all night, making sure she's still alive!"

Eliza did understand. "I do the same thing with Sophie, when she gets sick. I judge whether or not to take her to the doctor by how she acts. Is anyone else sick?"

"Thank goodness, no. How about yours?"

"We're all ok," Eliza didn't mention that she still had a stockpile of antiviral drugs at home – she didn't return them to the health department when she quit. "Hey, if you need anything, just come by ok? We should get together and hang out. Let our girls get together to play?"

"I'd like that," the woman said.

This is better, Eliza thought. This is normal. Neighbors arranging play dates.

A pile of newspapers lay in the walkway of the house on the other side of her. Why had she not noticed that before? No one came to the door when she rang the bell. She peeked through one of the windows and wondered if the owners were dead inside.

It took almost an hour to drive from Dalton to the diner. It was just outside of Cuero, a truck stop along the highway, attached to a run-down eight-room motel. While she'd prefer better accommodations, an expensive restaurant and a luxury hotel, Julia viewed her meeting with the mayor as an adventure: they undercover agents, meeting secretly under cover of darkness, hidden from spying eyes. Or at least hidden from his wife.

She arrived to an empty parking lot. A waitress sat on the sidewalk in front of the building smoking a cigarette, her apron in a wad on the concrete next to her.

"Hey!" Julia called to her as she approached. "Are you guys open?"

"Nope," the waitress said. She sucked on the cigarette and stared off at the highway.

"Oh. That's odd. I didn't expect you to be..."

"There's no truck today," the waitress interrupted. "No truck yesterday." She looked up at Julia's blank expression. "Food truck," she explained. "They aren't making deliveries. Ran out of food earlier today. They had to close up."

The waitress flicked ashes onto the sidewalk.

"I was supposed to meet someone here. A man? Have you seen him?" Julia checked her watch. A late man.

"Sorry sweetheart, I haven't seen anyone. Been waiting here for my own ride for a while now."

Julia checked her phone. No missed calls. No text messages. She tried calling him. His phone rang and rang.

A line of people snaked around the stadium. The first of them arrived around three in the morning – they would not be allowed inside until eight. They came with their lawn chairs, frail elderly women wrapped in blankets, men dragging their oxygen tanks, a heavily pregnant woman with two sleepy, whiney, kids sitting on the sidewalk. By 6:30am, security stopped allowing newcomers to join the line; they were already over the allotment. People toward the end of the line were warned: there might not be enough vaccine. But they stayed on. Hopeful.

Grant himself didn't arrive until seven. This being the largest clinic – they planned to give out three thousand shots in the university's football stadium. He wore a heavy coat and carried an insulated mug of coffee. He felt bad for the people in the line. Frost sparkled on the lawn; it had been a cold night. He called the Salvation Army and asked them to bring one of their food trucks. The Sally could always be relied upon for hot coffee. Some blankets, too, if they had some. He heard a lot of complaints about having the shot clinic outdoors, people standing in the cold, but at least outside if anyone in line harbored H7N1 they would be less likely to spread it around.

He left the signs inside his truck that advertised the flu clinic. Certainly no need for that. His volunteers stood in a cluster near the south side of the stadium next to several boxes of supplies. He had the vaccine delivered by armed guards; they were already inside. The volunteers all wore the badges on red lanyards that they'd picked up at the EOC the night before. A larger percentage of them than Jack wanted were veterinarians. They paired the vets up with the human-health workers, at least until the vets got the hang of things. The health department would only allow them to do adults. Families with children and pregnant women all would go to one of the RNs. Grant found that humorous. Seems like anyone who routinely gave shots to cats could handle a screaming kid.

He rifled through one of the supply boxes for a bullhorn. "Good morning," he said to the volunteers. The thing squealed. "We need to get all of this stuff inside. There are also folding tables inside the truck, some of you need to get those too. I've got red vests inside one of the supply crates. Wear one at all times." One of the volunteers found them and started handing them out.

They set ten tables up across the center of the stadium for the vaccination lines. Five more at the entrance. That would be the triage center. Make sure no one was already sick. Make sure they all meet the criteria for the shot: elderly, pregnant, or already having a chronic condition. Of course, Grant thought, there is really no way to prove it. The liars would go through the line and the honest people who didn't meet the guidelines would be turned away.

They placed more tables behind the vaccination tables as a pharmacy. Three pharm techs furiously filled syringes with vaccine. The volunteers vaccinated each other. Last practice for the vets.

"We're gonna be orderly about this, folks," one of the security guards told the people waiting in line. Those who had been sitting gathered their things and stood. An ancient man stood near the front of the line, bent over a cane. Grant watched as a spot of wet widened at the man's crotch, soaking down his right leg. Grant looked away, not wanting to embarrass him. He'd be through the line soon enough.

It did all begin orderly enough. The first few people came in, made their way past triage, were vaccinated without event, and made their way back out of the stadium. When they exited, they got to witness the first trouble. People who had shown up at eight, like the TV told them to, found that no one would be allowed in line. A group of them yelled at the security guards, none of whom wanted to turn people away, but what choice did they have? There just wasn't enough. As they argued with the newcomers, no one noticed the woman with the over-sized backpack until she started to yell. "This is the end! Rapture is nigh!" her hands in the air, her fingers splayed. "Don't take the vaccine! It is of the Devil! God sent this plague upon the earth, and the righteous will survive!"

"Shut up, you wack job!" someone else in line yelled. A few people laughed, a nervous, tense chuckling.

"You will see! You will all see!" She clawed at a thick belt around her waist.

"She's got a bomb!" the man behind her shouted. A woman screamed. People pushed the line forward, trying to escape into the stadium, trying to get away from the suicide bomber, but not wanting to get out of line. An old lady fell down into the crowd, pushed flat on the asphalt. A man stepped on her arm. Another man landed on her back, his heavy boots crunching into her kidneys. She cried out, but her cries went unheard in the commotion. Someone else kicked her in the face, pulling away much of her skin from her skull. She grasped for their legs, pulled at their pants, desperate to save herself. They were hardly aware of the soft, sinking feeling under their feet as they trampled her to death.

"The end is nigh! The end is nigh!" the woman screeched. And then she exploded.

Hundreds of small steel balls sprayed into the crowd, along with bloodied bits of the bomber. Her hand and part of her arm landed near one of the security guards. Shrapnel embedded in his face, piercing his eye. The crowd pushed and yelled, as the metal bits penetrated the softness of their flesh. A child stood in the eye of the storm, unharmed, screaming.

"Holy crap!" One of the fire fighters in the EOC yelled loud enough to quiet the room. He hung up the phone. "There was a bomber at the university! Multiple casualties. Estimating thirty injured, at least nine dead. It's crazy over there. Dispatch has three boxes in route. Johnson, get a mutual aid request. Maclean, call Memorial and let them know multiple trauma victims are on the way. Where's that epidemiologist? Get her over to Memorial for intel!"

Julia watched the beehive of the EOC buzz again. She was done playing. She put on her jacket, picked up her purse and left unseen.

CHAPTER 8

Dalton, Texas
Total infected = 15,769
Total dead = 636

Grant liked this bar. Dark. Anonymous. The Horseshoe Lounge was not the kind of place a person went to hook up with someone soft and warm for the night. No, you went to the Horseshoe to be alone.

The loud music, when he listened closely, was rather depressing. He drank with the broken. Old men missing most of their teeth. A grossly unattractive woman guzzling cheap beer after beer. The mirrors behind the bar reflected it all back at him, and he did his best not to catch his own reflection. Here no one knew who he was. No one cared about him, what he did. Just another loser in the dark. Not the guy in charge of the vaccination clinic where all those people died in a blaze of glory.

Grant shuddered. He gulped at his drink, but he already felt numb. He became an emergency manager to save people, not to watch them die. God, what a mess it was too. They had to turn it all over to Crime Scene. Tape off the area. Of course the people wouldn't leave. They snaked that line back and forth on the other side of the stadium, business as usual. Still, he knew that a lot of them saw it, body parts strewn around like a child's playroom. Except these were not doll parts.

The woman from the end of the bar approached, sat down next to him. "Buy me a drink," she said.

He admired her audacity. He motioned for the bartender. "Another scotch," he said, rattling the ice in his cup, "and whatever the lady is drinking."

"Stacy. My name's Stacy," she said. "Tell me yours, handsome."

He grunted at her. "You're not really my type."

"In the dark, who cares? I can make you feel better. Promise." She placed her hand on his thigh and razed her fingernails up towards his crotch.

"What makes you think I'm feelin' bad?" He felt himself growing hard, despite himself. He could take her into the men's room. Fuck her. Yeah, that might make him feel better after all.

"Oh, honey, everyone who comes here is. Just look at your face in the mirror. You look like someone died."

He glanced at his reflection. "Someone did."

He tossed some money on the bar. "Not tonight, Stacy," he said, and walked away, leaving her alone with her beer.

The thick mist obscured Cromwell's vision, making the ghostly trees appear suddenly in front of him as he approached. A bird twittered somewhere overhead. He picked his way through the underbrush, the damp earth sucking at his feet. He carefully guarded his balance. He didn't want to be one of those idiots who shot themselves in the woods.

He came to this place every fall at the onset of deer season. Alone. He had his rituals, and followed them religiously. Expensive cigar smoked as he drove the old truck to the deer lease (this being the only time he ever smoked). A fine bottle of wine opened upon arrival at the cabin. And always an early morning start, predawn, when the cold damp air would practically freeze his nuts off.

The cabin had no electricity. No electronics. No buzzing, no beeping, no voices calling for his attention, his input, his conversation, consultation, consideration. Just the noises of the forest, expecting nothing of him, tolerating his intrusion. A big old woodstove for heat. The perfect escape.

He walked along the trail to the deer stand, the route engraved into his memory despite the fog. While he never admitted it out loud, the deer were the least important of his hunting rituals; he frankly didn't care if he got one or not.

He enjoyed the fresh morning air in his lungs. The clean pine-scented air. Pristine. Virus free. He climbed the slick metal ladder into the small room of the deer stand. The windows were each covered with a flap of canvas that he rolled up and tied at the top. From here he could sit and survey the woods below. Waiting for his prey to enter his view.

He sat in a cold metal chair, his gun in his lap, his backpack on the floor in the corner. Supplies for the day's hunt. Extra shells. A couple of knives. Rope. Canteen. Trail mix and a one-pound bag of peanut M&Ms.

Movement by the corn feeder caught his attention.

A ten-point buck stood a few feet from the feeder, his eyes surveying the area, nostrils sniffing at the air, muscles tensed to run. *He knows I'm here. But where? Where am I?* Cromwell raised his rifle, balanced the end on the window frame and looked through the crosshairs at his prey.

His heart quickened, pounding against his chest wall, his finger just barely touching the trigger. *Wait for it. Wait.* The deer took a tentative mouthful of corn, and Cromwell had a clear shot of its heart.

No, he thought. *No more death.* He lowered the gun just as carefully as he had raised it, and watched the animal feed on the corn.

AFTERWORD

Three of the city council members sat in high-backed chairs on a horseshoe-shaped platform. Each had a microphone on the table in front of him, so everyone in the hall could hear their words easily. The mayor sat at the center, his platform a step higher than the council members, a fact he liked to remind them of.

One council member's chair sat empty. Precinct three. A victim of the Indonesian flu. They had yet to fill the position.

Geoff stood at a podium below them. He poured himself a glass of ice water. An aide had thoughtfully left a pitcher and glass on the podium. He watched his hand with its slight shake as he lifted the glass to his mouth. His doctor said that it was likely permanent, a sequelae of H7N1. A parting gift.

"Mr. Robins," the mayor said. "Thank you for coming before us this evening. I would like to begin by commending you and the health department as a whole, for your tireless efforts during the trials of the last few months. Thank you." He began to clap, and others in the room joined him. The sound reverberated off the council chamber's walls, hurting Geoff's ears, their acute sensitivity another gift from his illness.

"Thank you," Geoff had to lean forward at an awkward angle for his voice to enter the microphone. "Ten weeks ago, a traveler from Indonesia came to the City of Dalton to attend a conference put on by our university," he stumbled over his words, and almost lost his place. He could talk to anyone, but hated giving speeches. "The traveler brought with him a deadly virus. A virus which quickly spread throughout our city." Geoff gave up trying to make a polished presentation, gave up trying to make eye contact with the council, and read directly from his typed speech. "Since then, Memorial hospital has treated over three thousand patients. We have 702 members of our community, our family, our friends, dead. That we know of. A few of them have been buried, but most are still being processed by the medical examiner. It will be some time before we have everyone out of the Madison High School gym. Based on attack rates for the virus, we estimate that ten percent of the city's population was infected with H7N1. That amounts to about 20,000 people. While that all sounds grim, we've done much better than other cities. We have identified many people who developed mild illness. They were able to ride out the infection at home, oftentimes without medical intervention, attended to by family and friends. Occasionally alone. During the sixth week of the outbreak, we administered 500 doses of vaccine to first responders. Two weeks ago, we gave out 10,000 doses to the general public. These doses were given to people who had not caught the virus, who were screened for risk factors associated with complications and death had they contracted H7N1. The immune compromised. Pregnant women. Infants and toddlers. In monitoring for adverse effects from the vaccine, we documented ninety seven people who developed complications. Thirty-one of these were life-threatening. Six people died from post-vaccination encephalitis. The high rates of adverse events makes us very reluctant to give any more vaccine out, although we have been told it will be a long time before any more is available anyway." His voice cracked. He paused to take a sip of his water.

"Schools began reopening this week. There's still a lot of parents who are scared to send their kids, and we lost some teachers. The loss in classroom days means that school will be in session this summer. The university scrapped the fall semester. They plan to reopen in the spring.

"Reports of new infections have dropped off dramatically, almost stopped. It is easy to think that we are in the clear now. But I would like to note that approximately 160,000 people in this city are still susceptible to H7N1. They have no immunity from recovered disease or vaccination. With that many people at risk, there is a high probability that we will go through this again."

"Excuse me, Mr Robbins, for interrupting, but how soon do you anticipate that happening?" one of the council members asked.

"There is no way of knowing. Most of the models we used back when we were planning for an influenza pandemic predicted that it would hit in two waves. Dalton rode the first. Rode it out pretty well. It remains to be seen how, or if, we will deal with a second. I can tell you that we lost many, many responders. Some of them are included in our list of dead. Many more simply walked away from it. And the ones who are left are exhausted. We are currently dealing with significant mental health issues. People are still mentally in crisis. Post-traumatic stress disorder. Depression. One health care worker who committed suicide. We will likely be coping with mental health issues for some time to come."

"What are your recommendations? How should we move forward?" asked the mayor.

"That we continue heightened awareness and surveillance for new outbreaks. Enhanced basic hygiene. Scrupulous attention to hand hygiene in particular. We still have infected people in the community. They can act as a reservoir for the virus. People must protect themselves, they must take personal responsibility. The healthcare system cannot do everything. We need to continue limiting opportunities for large crowds and gatherings. Especially indoors. And people who are sick must be encouraged, must be allowed by schools or employers, to stay home during the course of their illness. We have to support people in this. Stay home if you are sick. At the health department, we will continue surveillance for new cases and areas of concern. And when we do get more vaccine, hopefully it will be safer vaccine, we will administer it as widely as possible."

"Thank you Mr. Robbins, for your report."

Geoff exited through the back of the building, succeeding in avoiding the press. He just wanted to go home.

ABOUT THE AUTHOR

Jessica Smartt Gullion, PhD, is Assistant Professor of Sociology at Texas Woman's University, where she teaches courses on medical sociology and qualitative research methods. Dr Gullion is the author of more than twenty peer-reviewed articles, in such journals as the *International Review of Qualitative Research*, the *Journal of Applied Social Science, Qualitative Inquiry, Infection Control and Hospital Epidemiology*, the *Archives of Internal Medicine*, and *Clinical Infectious Diseases*. Her research focuses on how communities cope with health threats.

ABOUT THE AUTHORS

Printed in the United States
By Bookmasters